STAND

STAND

LEARNING TO
LEAD *through* CONFLICT

Keep Standing!

TIMOTHY W. SLOAN

Dedicated to my wife Sonya.

Your love has allowed my fingertips to touch the grace of God.

"Each time a man stands up for an ideal, or acts to improve
the lot of others, or strikes out against injustice,
he sends forth a tiny ripple of hope,
and those ripples build a current which can sweep down
the mightiest walls of oppression and resistance."

SENATOR ROBERT F. KENNEDY
UNIVERSITY OF CAPE TOWN, SOUTH AFRICA,
JUNE 6, 1966

CONTENTS

ACKNOWLEDGEMENTS

I am grateful to sign my name to this work as the author, but it certainly belongs to a plethora of individuals. This process has been filled with its challenges, triumphs, sorrows and joys. Needless to say, the journey has been worth every step taken.

Thank you to the men and women who have helped to shape my fundamental beliefs and professional maturation. I am the product of sacrifices made by numerous coaches, teachers, professors, deacons, pastors, family and friends who invested heavily in me.

My ministerial launching pad has been made possible by my "Pauline figure," Rev. William A. Lawson. Your love for God, people and community inspires me to be a better leader every day. Special thanks to you and Mrs. Audrey Lawson for bringing us in to "groom us" and then sending us out to "grow us."

I am grateful to Dr. Marcus D. Cosby, who was the first respondent to my crisis of conflict and has stood beside me every step of the way. I have not known a day in pastoral ministry without your friendship, fraternal bond and ministerial support. Dr. Ralph Douglas West gave me meaningful words of encouragement throughout my journey. I have hung tightly to every word you have offered to me. Dr. Deforest B. Soaries, Jr. entered my life at a critical period in this process. Your demonstration of leadership and supportive conversations has meant the world to me. Special thanks to the many pastors I count as friends who stood with me throughout this entire process. Your support has been invaluable and your friendship beyond rewarding.

Every pastor needs a therapist they can talk to. I happen to have one of the best in Dr. Verdi Lethermon. Thank you for helping me to believe I could stand through it all.

As the birthing time for *Stand* approached, I was gifted with the expertise of some incredible people. Ramone Harper helped to orchestrate the completion of this project. Your friendship and support has helped me see the distant future with the clarity of a thumbprint. Johnny Stephens, your publishing expertise rolled us into the delivery room and facilitated every step of the process. Thank you for believing in this project and seeing it through. Ms. Dee McClendon, you are more than professional support, you are family. Thank you for catching and completing what I didn't even know needed to be done. I would be hard pressed to find someone as loyal as you.

A leader is only as good as the staff that surrounds him/them. I know for certain that I serve along side one of the best there is in kingdom building. Thank you for your love, support and covering throughout this entire process. I am especially grateful for the giftedness of Rev. Anthony L. Riley. You are more than a gift; you are one of God's great investments.

This book is the result of the privilege God has afforded me to serve one of the greatest churches in the country—The Luke. You have stood with me and believed in me throughout seasons of great change. *Stand* isn't possible without you. Thank you for believing that the vision I offered you was one worth following. Your love, encouragement and prayers have propelled me higher than you will ever know. Together we will continue to build bridges for future generations.

I am not here without two women who gave me a ladder to the moon and told me to climb. My mother Patricia Lowell is my biblical Hannah. You sacrificed everything to give me a fighting chance at life. I have lived every day of my life with the hope of making you proud. My late grandmother Julia Young Alberty helped shape my faith as a child. I can only imagine what it will be like to hug her again one day in the halls of eternity. Thank you to my entire family whose "bended knees" helped to bring us through.

To Sarah Julia, Soren Grace and Timothy John who gave their father uninterrupted time to write for an extended period. When I came home each day bearing the bruises of *leading through conflict*, your hugs helped speed up the healing process. Your daily question, "Daddy, is the book finished yet?" pushed me closer each time you posed it.

Lastly, I am thoroughly convinced that God lends out a special angel every now and then for kingdom impact and human companionship. I am a direct benefactor of that distribution program with the gift of my amazing wife, Sonya. I would not be half the man I think I am without you in my life. Thank you for believing in me and seeing more in me than I ever knew existed. You have truly taught me what it means to stand. Having you by my side is the joy of my life. Let's climb the stairs of eternity together and kiss the stars along the way—one by one.

Timothy W. Sloan

FOREWORD

This book is not a novel, not the product of a vivid imagination, not the ingenious creation of a skilled word-engineer whose research produced a story that seizes your attention through a romance or a crime or an adventure. This book is the fruit of the painful experience of a man of God who was, and still is, determined to use the superlative gifts with which God has endowed him, not to aggrandize himself, but to glorify God. *Stand* is the remarkable perspective of a pastor who has all the potential to be a rock star in a mega-church, but chooses to see faith as a calling, not as a red carpet career.

Dr. Timothy Sloan is pastor of The Luke Church in Humble, Texas. It is important to know that Dr. Sloan bears the credentials of a major university professor: Morehouse College (Alma Mater of Dr. Martin Luther King, Jr.), Princeton Theological Seminary, Rutgers University School of Law, Oxford University, the American University in Paris, and Colgate Rochester Crozer Divinity School, from which he received his Doctor of Ministry degree. He also has studied law in both New Jersey and Houston. Most black Baptist preachers claim the title "Doctor," but when you call Timothy Sloan "Doctor," you are absolutely accurate. Add to that sterling background his choice of a wife, a gorgeous M.D., First Lady of The Luke, Dr. Sonya Sloan, and an additional source of their pride (or gratitude to God), three to carry on the Sloan legacy—Sarah Julia, Soren Grace and Timothy John.

So with that kind of bio, what is Dr. Sloan doing struggling with the characteristic headaches of the pastorate? The answer to that question is the polestar of this book.

Dr. Sloan aptly defines the challenges we face in fulfilling our God-given purpose, and calls us to respond to our adversaries according to the model of Jesus, whose adversaries executed Him. Jesus came into conflict deliberately, driven by the will of His Father. He could have been adored by the masses, but shunned mass applause to preach a gospel that guaranteed opposition. He could have destroyed His opponents with a word, but this book calls us to examine and follow the pattern set by Jesus in "leading through conflict."

"Pastor." The term means "shepherd," and refers to one who is responsible for a flock. It is not synonymous with "preacher." Timothy Sloan was called to be a preacher, but to be a pastor requires tenacity beyond the calling; it requires facing and dealing with conflict. Dr. Sloan was superbly trained to be a preacher. But as the members of The Luke know (any who have been there for more than a decade), his sermons have evolved from eloquent delivery to paternal and prophetic counsel of a shepherd. And that evolution has developed in the midst of conflict, not from outsiders, but from members, even congregational leaders.

Stand describes Dr. Sloan's response to the opposition he faced upon laying out a vision for the church shortly after he was called there as pastor. That vision proved to be the catalyst for a series of conflicts. Those of us who know Timothy and Sonya Sloan have seen them deal with numerous battles, and we have marveled at how God, in the midst of it all, has blessed their leadership from the building of a new sanctuary to growing its membership to more than 6,000.

There are three key themes in this superb work:

- Following Jesus means battle—absolutely guaranteed.
- A pastor is responsible to a flock.
- God blesses the leader in the midst of conflict.

This is one of those books you need to place within arm's reach. You will return to it repeatedly.

William A. "Bill" Lawson, Pastor Emeritus
Wheeler Avenue Baptist Church – Houston, TX

—

INTRODUCTION

Difficulties are meant to rouse, not discourage.
The human spirit is to grow strong by conflict.

WILLIAM ELLERY CHANNING

As I sat on the stage waiting to speak, I kept thinking, "How in the world did I get in this position? How did it all come to this?" Outwardly, I appeared poised—my expression fixed like flint to the wind. Inwardly, I felt as if I was falling apart into a hundred pieces. My mind swirled as I recalled the events of the previous months. I thought I was on the right track and had led this church in the direction God wanted, only to find myself in a battle I didn't see coming.

Soon, the choir would finish and I would take the podium and deliver one of the most important messages of my life. The excitement in the room was palpable, but I was anything but excited. A great tension consumed me. I loved and cared for this church deeply; as their pastor, I had the privilege of watching God work miracles and change lives in countless individuals, families and communities. However, lurking among these sheep were wolves. They looked and talked like sheep, but their actions behind the scenes were deceptive and malicious. Not only did they want me out as senior pastor, they wanted to destroy me personally. I could sense them watching me from the crowd, licking their chops and hoping for my demise.

Suddenly, irrational thoughts started to fill my mind: "Why did I even accept the job here? I wouldn't be in this mess had I said, 'Thanks, but no thanks' and stayed at my previous job. That was at least comfortable and predictable. But this job? This is a fool's errand. The easiest thing to do would be to pack it up and leave."

The choir's final song was nearing an end and I surveyed the sea of people in front of me. So much of the experience made it seem like any other Sunday at our church. Senses were heightened and the feeling in the air was electric. The joyful singing and resounding praise that filled the place was familiar to me. Celebration reverberated throughout the auditorium and people were dancing in the aisles. Clearly, God's presence was in this place and I felt it. While so many were experiencing holy revelry, I sat sulking in my own cynicism towards the whole ordeal. "How can I celebrate with shouts to the Lord when it looks like his vision for me and our church is coming apart at the seams?"

In the past, whenever I was frustrated or facing a big challenge, I would do what I knew I could do, which is *preach!* Whenever I preach, a passion is fueled within me and I come to life. The pulpit was my safe haven, and the place I knew I could have some modicum of control when it seemed like the world around me was chaotic. Without a doubt, the past few months felt out of control at The Luke and I thought the church might come off the rails at a moment's notice.

I was confident I was being obedient with the vision God gave me for our church. But so much had happened to threaten that vision. At the time, I thought the math was pretty simple in carrying out God's work: vision + obedience = blessing and fulfillment. Looking back, I see that God wanted to take me beyond that simplistic understanding. He was taking me on a journey that would teach me more about leadership than I ever thought possible. And I was learning a valuable lesson in leadership—that a leader cannot please everyone, but he or she is sure to have conflict with someone. Through this experience I began to identify with the difficulties, frustrations, setbacks and needs of others so prolific in Scripture.

The choir concluded and my moment had arrived. I scanned the crowd and noticed a group of teenagers in a corner of the auditorium. Normally, I'd see them passing notes or making funny remarks to their friends about others being emotional during the service. It wasn't uncommon to see them space out or be entirely disinterested. Today was different. They looked at me with a fixed focus that caught me off guard. I had never seen such arrested attention from them before.

> A LEADER CANNOT PLEASE EVERYONE, BUT HE OR SHE IS SURE TO HAVE CONFLICT WITH SOMEONE.

That glance happened in a flash, but it unlocked something powerful in me. The message was clear: God had a purpose and he wanted me at The Luke. I was called to lead this church—through thick and thin—and influence the next generation. If I shirked my responsibilities by tucking tail and running away, I would be outside God's will. I would be like Jonah, who ran from God's clear instructions for him to preach in Nineveh (Jonah 1:1-3). Jonah's disobedience jeopardized the salvation of the Ninevites, but his eventual obedience to God's will led to the repentance and salvation of the capital of the Assyrian Empire (Jonah 3:1-10).

I knew I couldn't run. What was happening in our church was bigger than me. This was God's vision and I knew he would carry it out through us. Our church had been down a rocky road with obstacles around every bend in the past months. The room was hushed with the silence of anticipation; a multitude of men and women of all generations were on the edge of their seat, anxiously waiting on what I would say. The stage lights were bright and hot. A bead of sweat rolled down my forehead. I wiped it off with my handkerchief and opened my Bible. In that moment I wasn't nervous. Nor was I scared. I knew what I had to do, regardless of the difficulties and conflict that lie ahead for our church. I was going to *preach*. And I was going to stand!

LEADERS AFFECT CHANGE

This book is my story. I didn't choose it, but I lived it and learned a lifetime's worth of lessons from it. *Stand* is my attempt to put on paper what God has taught me through an experience I believe you can relate to on some level as a leader.

Being a pastor often feels like you're spinning multiple plates at the same time. The church—like any organization—is full of broken people with different wants, needs and desires. Trying to address all of these and steer an organization in the right direction is a tall order for anyone, even the best of leaders.

> REAL AND LASTING CHANGE DOESN'T HAPPEN WITHOUT SOME DIFFICULTY, BECAUSE HUMAN BEINGS TEND TO GRAVITATE TOWARDS WHAT'S COMFORTABLE, KNOWN AND SAFE.

Great leaders influence others towards change, but change hardly ever comes easily. More often than not, change is an uphill climb that requires patience and conviction to shift previously held beliefs and dispositions of others and show them a better way of thinking and living. Real and lasting change doesn't happen without some difficulty, because human beings tend to gravitate towards what's comfortable, known and safe. When you disrupt the status quo (i.e., the way things have always been done in an organization), you can expect some pushback. It's likely that some in your organization will openly oppose you.

I'm confident many of you reading this can think of a person (or group) that has resisted your leadership and ideas. Conflict is a common occurrence in all walks of life. So we shouldn't be surprised when we come up against it in our day-to-day lives. Being a leader requires that we lean into conflict rather than run from it. Being a great leader on any level means being responsible to address and deal with conflict in order to affect real and lasting change.

LEADERS HAVE VISION

You might think godly people would all get behind a leader's God-directed vision. As much as we would like that to be true, that's not the reality we often experience. Even the early church had to wrestle through conflict. The early church was a diverse group of cultures and traditions. Is it any wonder that there was plenty of disagreement among those first Christians? That being said, Acts also shows us that God works within people's differences and disagreements to bring about his will.

God is not deterred by conflict and uses it to fulfill his purposes. He does that through leaders who carry out his vision. Great leaders are men and women of vision. They are able to see beyond what is to what could be. Great leaders are able to navigate the icebergs of conflict to lead a group or organization into great horizons of possibility and effectiveness. Successful leaders are those that are able to connect others to the vision he or she has received from God. God gives leaders his vision and leaders are responsible to point others to it by influencing and inspiring others to go with them into new and uncharted territory.

NO SHORT CUTS IN LEADERSHIP

There is no short cut on the road to becoming the kind of leader that leaves a legacy. God doesn't equip his leaders that way. Just look at God's leaders in Scripture. Their paths weren't smoothly paved highways. They were wrought with all kinds of conflict, disappointment, frustration and obstinacy from those that followed them. The challenge for those leaders—and every leader—is using those difficult experiences constructively.[1] This is especially true in the area of conflict.

Conflict is a necessary part of the leadership journey and cannot be avoided. Sooner or later, conflict will find us in our relationships, workplaces and ministries. Making the decision to stand when conflict arises will set you apart as a true leader and difference maker for others.

I didn't learn leadership by taking a class. I learned it by experience, which is where we all discover whether we're cut out for leadership. Leadership in any field comes with a high degree of difficulty and no guarantees. Personally, I wouldn't trade being a pastor for anything, despite the difficulties. To be sure, I've had my fair share of sleepless nights, hardship, suffering and difficult relationships. However, the wonderful thing about our God is that he used those experiences to make me a better leader. Never, in my wildest dreams as a bright-eyed seminarian, did I imagine that carrying out God's vision would be such a challenge.

AN APPOINTMENT WITH ADVERSITY

If you want to make a difference in your world, get ready for some adversity. Without adversity, our lives are prone to become synthetic representations of what we call 'life.' We may avoid the deep valleys of suffering that come with living in this world, but avoiding adversity comes with a price: forfeiting the flourishing life and incalculable joys God intended for those who take a stand for him.

God taught me to stand through adversity. The leader I am today is a direct result of the refining fire of adversity that God allowed me to experience. Dealing with adversity and conflict is part of the job description for leaders. Like a master craftsman creating a warrior's sword, he molds and shapes us into the kind of leaders that will stand in the face of adversity. The blows of his hammer can be painful, but they make us stronger and more equipped to withstand the fight and triumph once we enter into battle.

Stand is the story of how I learned to lead others in the midst of conflict and adversity. I want to give you the full picture of what I've experienced and learned as a leader. In these pages you'll read stories when I succeeded through obedience. You'll also read stories where I missed the mark and had to learn the hard way.

I'm inviting you into my intimate space to see the portrait of a man trying to understand what it means to be a leader who leaves a legacy. My desire is for you to come away from reading this book celebrating a God who calls leaders and equips them to do extraordinary things. I hope you see that growing into a successful leader means influencing others towards transformation and real change.

Stand is a story about committing to a vision, despite the odds and opposition. It's about owning your convictions and seeking to be faithful, even when times get tough. It's about surrendering to a God-directed vision that will out-live you. *Stand* is about serving others and seeking a better future for them above personal accolades.

While *Stand* is my story, I know I'm not the first (or the last) to go down this road. There are countless stories across history of men and women taking a stand for Christ and seeking his approval rather than man's. In Hebrews 11 the author chronicled the faithfulness of God's people to encourage his readers, because he knew that stories have the power to inspire and cause us to believe a greater life and future are possible. But he didn't want his leaders to simply listen to those stories. He wanted those stories to lead to action. He wanted his readers to stand.

THE BEGINNING OF THE STORY

The story of *Stand* began with me accepting the call to pastor an historical and very traditional church in Humble, Texas. The church had a rich heritage and long-standing presence in the community. In many respects the church seemed stable, but I could sense that something was missing. The fires of passion for life-changing ministry were ebbing low among the congregants there.

I launched into my position with a vision for change to grow the church beyond its four walls and ultimately impact the global world. My conviction was that God had entrusted me with this vision and was calling me to hold the flag in leading this body of believers into new and exciting territory. Overall, I wanted to shift the church from a more traditional model of ministry to an emerging model that would address the present-day needs and perspectives of our members. I love tradition, but often it can lead to traditionalism (a form of religion that is legalistic and overly dependent on methods and rituals that are devoid of spiritual power). I feared our church was on that path and that we needed to make a change in direction.

The first four years of ministry were incredibly fruitful. Things progressed well, and we experienced our fair share of challenges along the way. I felt God's favor as I gained ground as a pastor and community leader. In this season I was developing greater depth and understanding of God's Word as I preached week in and week out. My eyes were keenly focused and my hands ready to do more work for the Lord and the people he gave me to lead. We were accomplishing things and seeing God bless our church in many ways. We were growing at a fast rate and it was only a matter of time before we needed more space. Along with the church's leadership, we started to entertain the idea of building a new facility to accommodate our ever-increasing congregation.

BEING A GREAT LEADER ISN'T ABOUT PLEASING EVERYONE. IT'S ABOUT PLEASING GOD AND CARRYING OUT HIS VISION.

I thought our church was right where it needed to be and that building a new facility was the appropriate and right decision. However, I didn't see clearly at the time that this was more than just changing the church's address. The direction I was taking the church involved more. It involved history, authority and that dreaded C-word—change. Many in our church had been members for generations. So much of their identity was wrapped up in our church building. To some degree, I understood that. We all want a place to belong—a relationship, group, organization or church that will welcome us in and give us an identity. Unfortunately, that desire can become warped over time as those identifying traditions give way to traditionalism. You can imagine the difficult task I had in getting this group to get on board with God's vision for this church! And you know as well as I do that encouraging people who are set in their ways to change is as difficult a task as any.

I knew this was not going to be easy, but I was prepared to roll up my sleeves and try to persuade thousands of people to look within themselves (and to the Lord) and consider the bigger picture. I wanted to walk this congregation lovingly and patiently through this process, because it was a big change for them. The conflict that ensued after I shared my vision for growth at The Luke was about more than building a new building on a new property. (Although that became the most argued point.) It was about the fears that vision stirred up—fears of leaving the old and familiar, resentments about being told what to do by "some young pastor," anxieties about position and security. The proposal for *new* and *different* disrupted generations of tradition and it placed me in the middle of a heated battle. My impression was that, in time, the old guard would come to their senses and see that this was better for everyone. However, when I announced that we were going to build our new church on a different property, many thought I had signed the death certificate to the church.

The next six years brought new and greater challenges for our church. We lost and gained many in those six years. In fact, we would grow twice our size. Through that season of growth I was learning that commitment to a vision means that you're likely to lose valuable relationships along the way. It's unfortunate, but that's the reality that real leaders have to come to terms with in leadership. Being a great leader isn't about pleasing everyone. It's about pleasing God and carrying out his vision.

THE STAND WITHIN

Never could I have imagined the spotlight that would be thrown on our church during this time. Soon, we would become the popular topic of barbershop and water cooler conversations and even in the headlines of local media outlets. The onslaught of attention we received was embarrassing and, honestly, I wished for it all to stop. This was not the kind of attention I wanted for the church and myself.

By day I was preaching and teaching to thousands, but at night I would go to battle with the fear, anxiety and depression that internally gripped me in this struggle. Often I would be awakened in the night with the thought, "Am I really just a failure?" The remarkable thing is that I've talked to many leaders who have experienced what I did. Perhaps you've had similar thoughts as a leader, spouse or parent. Sharing our insecurities and personal struggles isn't easy, especially for leaders. We're supposed to be the ones that have it all together, right? The truth is we don't have it all together. No one does. That's why we need God. That's why we need his wisdom and his direction to help us when it feels like the walls are closing in on us or that we've messed up and are beyond repair.

As a leader, you must take a stand within yourself against the voices that cause shame, doubt and lack of faith. Making the decision to stand will teach you and empower you to help others in need. Just because you deal with something like depression (as I did), doesn't mean you are any less of a leader. By God's grace, that experience gives you a platform to have a positive impact on many who are going through something similar.

As a pastor, I get an honest glimpse into the lives of many in my congregation. I've sat at the dinner table with many of our church's members who have shared personal struggles, hang-ups, addictions, conflicts, adversity, pain, grief and the like. Whenever they give voice to what they're going through, I often tell them, "I understand, because I've been there too." In this life we learn and grow together as a community of people in need of God's grace and direction.

This may come as a surprise to you, but dealing with conflict was the best thing that ever happened to me. It was God's gift to grow me as a leader. Each challenge presented a new opportunity for me to learn something new about myself and the beliefs I held on to for dear life. Conflict brought me greater depth and understanding of who God is and how he works. Through conflict I saw what it looks like to forgive others as Jesus did and love them without condition. I was also learning to forgive myself for past mistakes and poor choices. My growth didn't happen in an instant. Rather, growth happened daily as I encountered the challenges and conflicts of being a leader. Looking back I see that the biggest difference maker for me was my decision—no matter what happens or how bad things got—to stand!

THIS STORY IS FOR YOU

You might be a pastor or church leader like me. Maybe you're a business owner who oversees a number of employees, offices and projects. Maybe you're an executive for a non-profit charged with charting a new course for organizational purpose. Perhaps you're a stay-at-home mom who wants to raise her children right and set them up for success in life. If you're a leader in any capacity, this book is for you. *Stand* is my story and I hope it resonates with you because you understand the need to become a better and more effective leader and person. Leadership is more than just accomplishing things. It's about building your character to be strong and courageous in the face of difficulty and conflict. That's the kind of person God has made you to be.

This book is not a how-to, step-by-step manual for leadership. Beware of one-size-fits-all books on leadership; leadership and conflict are too complex and varied to have one "right" solution or approach. That's why I'm giving you guidelines and principles to live by in this book.

Stand is a story to show you the challenging and rewarding path every great leader must go down. If you've come with me this far, I encourage you to read further and discover what God wants to reveal to you about your own life and leadership through my story. Together, let's stand!

DISCUSSION QUESTIONS

1. Read Ephesians 6:13. In spiritual battles, Scripture calls us to stand. In what ways is standing an offensive position? In what ways is it defensive?

2. Spiritual conflict is often encountered when we are challenged to please God above pleasing people. In what ways has 'people pleasing' been a temptation for you? In what ways have you seen victory in this area?

3. What skills have you acquired to prepare you for leadership? How have those skills given you success in leadership?

4. What have been the biggest giants you have faced so far in leadership?

1

FIGHTING THE GOOD FIGHT

Nothing is given to man on earth—struggle is built into the nature of life, and conflict is possible—the hero is the man who lets no obstacle prevent him from pursuing the values he has chosen.

ANDREW BERNSTEIN

In my walk with the Lord I have encountered many giants. Of course, I'm not talking about Paul Bunyan here. I'm talking about spiritual giants that try to strike terror into the hearts of God's people. They can be people or situations that make us want to run away and cower in fear because of what we perceive them to be.

Now, the peculiar thing about these giants is that they seem larger and more threatening than they actually are. At first glance, giants present a challenge that seems insurmountable. We feel overmatched in the battle and wonder if it is wise to engage in the fight. When we face giants we need right perspective to see giants for what truly are. We get right perspective with our greatest weapon against these giants: faith.

Anyone in the military or martial arts will tell you that you need skill and acumen whenever you engage an opponent. You need to size-up your opponent and know what kind of fight you're getting into. You also have to be quick on your feet and have the wherewithal to make good decisions in a confrontation. One false step and your opponent, sensing a weakness, might overtake you. Therefore, we have to enter the fight and face our own giants with the right mind, skill and focus to be victorious.

KING JEHOSHAPHAT FACES HIS GIANTS

The Bible is full of stories of men and women facing down giants. The classic example is David's showdown with Goliath in 1 Samuel 17. There's also the story of Gideon leading God's people in victory over the Midianites in Judges 6-7. Another story I'd like to highlight is found in 2 Chronicles 20 where King Jehoshaphat led Judah's army into battle against three formidable enemies in the Ancient Near East.

Fresh winds of reform and revival were sweeping through Jerusalem and throughout the kingdom of Judah during Jehoshaphat's reign (2 Chron. 19). Judah was experiencing religious renewal from north to south. New judges and priests were appointed to restore order in the land. Jehoshaphat was bold in carrying out God's vision for his people. Everything seemed to be going well with King Jehoshaphat on the throne.

In the middle of this incredible time in Judah's history a giant appeared. Rather, three giants appeared. The Moabites, the Ammonites and the Meunites united their armies to go into battle against Judah. The deck was stacked against Judah; they were severely outnumbered in this fight.

How would King Jehoshaphat respond? How would he react to a fight he knew he couldn't win in his own power? As Judah's leader, Jehoshaphat did the right thing and petitioned God for help. He also called his people to do the same. He was confident that the God who rescued his people in times past could do it again. So he prayed for God to intervene. He didn't know how or when God would deliver them from their enemies, but he was resolved to stand and wait for God to give them the victory against seemingly unbeatable opponents.

Just like Jehoshaphat, we face giants in our lives on a daily basis. These giants try to keep us from doing God's will and want us to doubt the power that resides in us and for us (Rom. 8:31). We live in a culture that would prefer us to sit idly on the sidelines and not enter the fight. It uses fear and doubt to make us think the fight isn't worth it and is unwinnable. However, God calls you and me to stand in the midst of the giants that challenge us. As God's children, we have entered a fight with a very real enemy that wants to see us fail. You and I are called to face our enemies and fight the good fight of faith in order to see salvation and victory from the Lord.

> GOD HAS GIVEN YOU THE TOOLS AND PROMISES NECESSARY TO HANDLE WHATEVER SITUATION (OR GIANT) YOU'RE CURRENTLY FACING.

Taking a stand may sound passive when held up against our results-driven, overly aggressive culture. But that's exactly what God calls his people to do. Remember: God is the one that will deliver us and give us victory over these giants. We do not have it in our power to overcome the odds on our own. We need God's directing vision to guide us and his strength and wisdom to help us in the fight. If God has given you a vision for your life, don't panic because things aren't going according to plan or because you're facing opposition and setbacks. Has any vision of God ever gone according to our preconceived plans, timetables and expectations? Never! Instead, God wants to use our challenges to grow us into the kind of people that will trust him and stand for him, even when victory looks impossible. Be encouraged. God has given you the tools and promises necessary to handle whatever situation (or giant) you're currently facing.

A FOUNDATION IN LEADERSHIP

Becoming a great leader doesn't happen overnight. You don't just wake up one day ready to lead others in this world. What you can do is realize that God has used your life's story to prepare you to lead. A strong foundation in leadership begins by using the accumulation of experiences and opportunities that have equipped you with the skills and wisdom necessary to lead effectively.

When I look back on my childhood and adolescence, I see that I was being prepared for something. The wealth of experiences and relationships in those years helped fashion me into who I am today. I've had the privilege of going to some of the finest universities this country has to offer. Along the way I've sat at the feet of some of our nation's most gifted and influential leaders.

You would think this pedigree would put me on the fast track as a leader. While I'm grateful for those opportunities, I know that they didn't fully prepare me for leadership outside the classroom and lecture hall. I think you would agree that life itself is our greatest teacher. Life's experiences instruct us and train us like no textbook ever can.

I'm a big boxing fan. When I see a boxer in training I marvel at their level of commitment. Boxers rigorously prepare their mind and body to face their opponent. Daily they discipline themselves by training and studying their opponent's style and technique. But the best boxers (the ones that actually win fights!) are the ones that utilize their training and preparation to successfully execute inside the ring.

THE RUMBLE IN THE JUNGLE

Execution is simply putting into effect a plan of action. When you execute, you're translating your plans and preparation into reality and action. Being a great leader is more than just having good ideas; successful leaders are more than just planners and dreamers. The best leaders I've seen are the ones that use their skill and expertise to execute a plan of action. How we fight in leadership will determine whether we win or lose.

One of my favorite fights is the *Rumble in the Jungle*, a 1974 rematch between Muhammad Ali and George Foreman in Zaire, Africa. The odds were stacked against the once dominant Ali. Foreman was younger and stronger and known for his thundering punches. Many thought Ali was past his prime and didn't have a chance against Foreman.

But Ali had a plan and developed an innovative strategy against Foreman that might give him the victory. To execute this plan Ali would have to adjust his fighting style, using the ropes to support him while Foreman punched him repeatedly and used up his energy. This technique came to be known as 'rope-a-dope.' The strategy proved successful and Ali, with little resistance, was able to capitalize with a counterattack when Foreman ran out of gas. Eventually, Ali was able to knock out Foreman and win the fight. His strategy worked because it was executed with skill and precision. After the fight, when a reporter asked Ali if he thought he would win the fight, Ali told him he knew if he was still standing in the fourth round after Foreman hit him as hard as he could, he would win the fight.

> EXECUTION IS SIMPLY PUTTING INTO EFFECT A PLAN OF ACTION.

Of course, the fights I experienced growing up weren't on the scale of the *Rumble in the Jungle*, but they were nevertheless significant in teaching me how to stand and not back down in the face of my opponent. I remember a fight when I was younger where, by all accounts, my opponent was bigger, faster and stronger than I was. In a matter of moments our playground became Madison Square Garden as our friends cheered us on. Just as the fight was about to start, my friend took me aside. He said to me, "He's just a bully and not much of a boxer. All you've got to do is stand up to him. If you don't back down, you'll walk away a winner." I took my friend's advice and walked away the winner that day. Putting his advice into practice, I proved to myself early in life that no matter the size of the challenge, I would stand my ground and face it.

My days of dealing with bullies didn't end on the playground. Years later I would find myself in a fight that would become one of the most defining moments of my life. It would become a golden opportunity for me to take a stand for what was right against my giants. While the odds were not in my favor, I knew I would not quit and I drew from my preparations and experiences to skillfully execute a plan that would bring victory.

THE BEGINNING OF SOMETHING BIG

King Jehoshaphat wanted God's best for Judah. He put in place reforms that would ensure justice, establish order and encourage revival in the land. He wanted to please God and he trusted that God would give him favor in leading his people. Like all good kings, he cared for his people and wanted them to experience peace and prosperity.

Like Jehoshaphat, I wanted to lead our church to experience peace and prosperity as I attempted to institute changes that would take us in that direction. The church was growing rapidly and we were running out of room to seat everyone coming to our Sunday services. We had to utilize the fellowship hall of our church to accommodate the overflow of people we had.

To address our growing pains, I decided to use a biblical approach from the life of Moses. Just as Moses organized God's people for their journey into the Promised Land by commissioning leaders among the twelve tribes, I put together a team of church leaders to help me during this season of growth and change. After performing a long and in depth study, they reported to me their findings. To address our need for space, we had two options: 1) purchase more property at our current location and build on to the church, or 2) find a new location that had enough land to build a facility to accommodate our growing congregation. It didn't take long for us to realize that the second option was best for the church.

We spent the subsequent weeks and months scouting possible locations. I'll admit that I'm no real estate expert, but I was convinced that when we found the place God wanted for us, he would make it clear to me. One day I received a call from one of the team members telling me, "Pastor, I think we've found it!"

She could barely contain her excitement. Neither could I. As soon as I could, I got in my car and drove to the location. Standing on that property for the first time remains a vivid memory in my mind. It was a huge moment for me personally. I had labored tirelessly to get us to this point and that property made it seem that we were coming close to fulfilling God's vision for our church. That being said, I didn't want to jump the gun and assume this was the right property. After all, I had to consider the church and its leadership in the decision. Moreover, this decision would affect so many people and it would take our church in a new direction that would extend beyond my leadership and lifetime.

> **PREPARING OTHERS FOR CHANGE REQUIRES A MULTI-FACETED APPROACH TO YOUR LEADERSHIP.**

Our leadership deliberated and came to a decision to move forward, purchase the new property and share our decision with the church body. We were riding a wave of momentum and I was certain this was God's will for us and that there would be little resistance to our plans. We held a business meeting to vote on the decision to purchase the property. Those involved in the meeting overwhelmingly supported the plan and voted in favor of it. We were finally closing in on making God's vision a reality.

King Jehoshaphat was obedient in carrying out God's vision by bringing much-needed change and reform to Judah, but he wasn't without enemies. Such is the case for any leader looking to make a significant difference. Despite the best of intentions for God's people, Jehoshaphat would run up against serious opposition. In my situation I knew I would have detractors in leading our church to undertake an enormous change. However, I couldn't imagine that people would resist with such vehemence because of my desire to grow our church.

How does a leader respond to resistance? There are healthy and unhealthy ways to respond. You could move ahead with your plans, fully convinced you are right, and disregard your detractors as ignorant and out-of-step. That, of course, would be an unhealthy approach. A better (and healthy) way to approach resistance would be to consider the following steps:

- Seek to understand the different perspectives involved.
- Listen carefully to all sides.
- Identify the main issue or cause of the conflict.
- Confront any and all conflict quickly.
- Address the conflict openly and mutually agree on a solution.

As far as I was concerned, we had gone about this decision the right and diplomatic way. We showed care and listened to those in favor of and against the decision. Considering the overwhelming support from the majority of members, I believed this was a small roadblock along an otherwise clear path. Little did I know that I was about to enter a fight unlike any other I had experienced to that point.

After the decision to buy the property and build a new facility was approved, I assumed that was it. The hard work had paid off and our church was heading in the right direction under my leadership. I dreamed of Houston—and all of Texas—hearing about the great things happening at our church and praising God for them. I went into my office to sit, reflect, pray and thank God for what he had done. I was looking forward to the coming years and moving our church into our own Promised Land. I felt at peace and was sure we were embarking on a joyful and extraordinary journey. Unfortunately, that peace would not last for long.

PREPARING FOR CHANGE

In leading our church as pastor, I knew it was necessary to shepherd people well through this transition. Granted, we were only moving four miles down the road, but it was apparent that this would not be as simple as packing a few boxes and renting a U-Haul. Our visibility would change—no longer would we be a small, familiar community church. Moses prepared the Israelites to enter the Promised Land. In like manner, leaders must prepare those who follow them for changes and difficulties ahead. Preparing others for change requires a multi-faceted approach to your leadership.[1]

How does a leader prepare others for change? Consider the following steps in leading a successful transition:
- Communicate the change clearly.
- Present a strategy for moving forward.
- Lead from the front and by example.
- Acknowledge the importance of others.
- Share the benefits (personal and corporate) of the change.

To help with the transition, I began a series of sermons on the Book of Nehemiah called *Bridging the Gap*. It was the perfect biblical illustration of God's people dealing with change and transition in order to carry out God's will. Weekly I would be emboldened by Nehemiah's faith and ability to lead God's people during a difficult season. Ironically, the events that would soon play out in our church would mirror Nehemiah's story in uncanny ways. It became a running joke in our church that, if you wanted to know what was happening at our church, you just needed to turn to the next chapter in Nehemiah!

THE DAY THAT CHANGED EVERYTHING

It was on a September day in 2006 when my story took an unexpected turn. At first, it felt like a normal Sunday. I preached at both church services and got a jubilant response from our congregation. Throughout those services I had an uneasy feeling; it was that feeling in the pit of your stomach that something just isn't right. After the service I visited with some of our members and retreated to my office. A few minutes later I heard a loud banging on my door. Into my office marched three, stern-faced deacons from the church. They handed me a folded piece of paper and, before I could read it, they told me, "Your services are no longer needed here."

I was dumbfounded. I could not believe this was happening. The rug was taken from right under me. My immediate thought was, "After all I have done for this church, after all the sacrifices I have made to better this church, you're firing me? Is this really how you treat someone for doing the right thing?" It felt like a bad dream that I couldn't wake up from.

Perhaps the thing that hurt the most was that these deacons stood by me and were my biggest supporters in the past. I considered them close friends. In the past they had helped me in difficult seasons and encouraged my leadership in the church and community. Now, without warning or explanation, they were betraying me. My heart sank as I sat there and looked at them in utter bewilderment.

The plot of my story had taken a sharp turn. Instead of preparing our church for change, I was getting ready to engage in a battle I didn't plan on fighting. The moment was intense and emotions were running high. I needed to take decisive action. How do I respond after I've been personally attacked and undermined and my future is hanging in the balance? A foolish decision would have lasting implications on my family, our church and me. Based on the advice of wise counsel, I decided to call an emergency church meeting.

That evening hundreds of our members showed up for the meeting. I shared what had happened and made a pledge to them to fight this and take a stand for what I believed was the right thing to do. In a powerful demonstration of support, one-by-one they stood up and said they would support me. The chorus of prayers and comforting words in that room for my family and me was truly humbling. I felt their support and I knew they were looking to me to be the leader that wouldn't run from this conflict. There was more than just my job on the line. The future of this church was at stake. I had decided: the fight was on.

DECIDE TO STAND

I was aware that taking a stand wouldn't happen without resistance. It never does. A small group had conspired to railroad this decision to grow the church into a new building and property. They were determined to fight any and all who were for change. This group obtained a restraining order to keep me off the church's property. That led to a battle in court where the judge ruled in my favor and the restraining order was lifted. As my supporters and I exited the courthouse in victory we were met with the bright lights of news cameras. We were the leading story in Houston as anchors referred to our fight as one of "biblical proportions."

I began to wonder, "How did I go from thinking I was doing what was right to having to defend myself to reporters?" I had seen my fair share of churches that experienced in-fighting and conflict. I never imagined it would happen to our church. We were the talk of the town and not for reasons I was happy about.

In order to be a successful leader in conflict, it's important to remember these key ideas:

- Determine why you are fighting. What is the battle about?
- Put the battle in its proper perspective. What effect will this battle have on you, those who follow you, your community and others who may be watching?
- How you fight will determine whether you win or lose. Will power alone will not determine who wins. Rather, it is the willingness to stand in the face of adversity that will make you triumphant.

IT'S BIGGER THAN YOU

I began to see that these events—as crazy and chaotic as they may have seemed at the time—were ordained by God and had a purpose. We were part of a bigger story that was being played out. While my face was all over the news, I knew I wasn't the main character in this story. God was. That's when the weight started to lift off my shoulders. I found strength again to fight the coming battles and stand. I was still responsible to lead our church and direct everyone's focus on God and his will.

Navigating your way through conflict can be overwhelming. Know that you're not alone. Leaders everywhere deal with the weight of responsibility that comes with leadership. God wants you to be able to stand in the midst of conflict and adversity. I'd like to share seven principles that have helped me along the path of leadership:

1. Cast the Vision
2. Define the Conflict
3. Seek the Right Guidance
4. Create a Battle Plan
5. Lead with Purpose
6. Face Your Fears
7. Embrace Recovery and Restoration

In the following chapters, we'll discover how (when put into practice), these will help you fight the good fight of faith. They will be the stones and slingshot you need in battle, because every fighter needs some tried-and-true weaponry and defensive strategies for victory.

DISCUSSION QUESTIONS

1. As a leader, how can you prepare others for change in your organization?

2. What have been some of the biggest battles you've faced in leadership?

3. What was your source of strength in those battles? How did it help you in your leadership?

4. Review the seven leadership principles we will discuss in this book. At first glance, which do you feel you most strongly posses? Which are areas of weakness?

2

CAST THE VISION

Leadership is the capacity to translate vision into reality.

WARREN BENNIS

I t is extremely difficult to accomplish anything without vision. Vision opens our imagination to see greater possibilities of achieving something worthwhile and significant in life. It directs every brushstroke of an artist creating something beautiful on her canvas. Every blow of a sculptor's chisel on an unformed piece of marble is determined by it. A master chef works for hours in a kitchen with a set of tools, multiple ingredients and a vision of something delicious to come out of the oven. Everyone needs a vision to excel. Leaders in every field plan their next steps and movements based upon a clear vision.

I think you're with me in saying that I won't follow anyone without vision. More than just excite, a vision directs. It gives an end goal of something to be achieved, but it also suggests that much work must be done to bring it to fruition. A vision needs a clear path; you can't meander your way towards accomplishing a vision. Of course, there will be missteps along the way, but a clear vision of a goal that's always present in your mind will make the journey worthwhile.

A KING WITH VISION

Scripture tells us that King Jehoshaphat was a man of vision. He was instrumental in tearing down the altars in Judah dedicated to foreign gods and returning the hearts of the people back to God. He chose the righteous path and held God's people accountable for their rebellious actions against God. He reminded the people of God's vision for them; that he expected them to walk in right standing with him, worship him with sincere hearts and enjoy the fruits of a God-centered life. Among Judah's leadership, Jehoshaphat laid out a vision for greater things to his generals, judges and priests to implement.

Jehoshaphat's command to all of Judah was clear and profound: "You must serve faithfully and wholeheartedly in the fear of the Lord" (2 Chron. 19:9). He followed that command with an encouraging call for Judah to "act with courage and may the LORD be with those who do well." Jehoshaphat knew what God expected of him as a leader of his people. He was called to put God's people back on the right track and to serve God instead of idols.

Like all great leaders, Jehoshaphat was a leader for his time. God raised him up to accomplish something special and unique for that particular season in Judah's history. Likewise, you are a leader for this present hour and God can use you to accomplish great things for his name. If you are to lead well, you need a clear vision and the courage to implement it. A vision is worthless without the courage to work towards it in the face of great obstacles and difficulties that are sure to come your way.

God strategically equips people for leadership, because he has an expected result in mind. Every leadership journey begins with an intended destination. As a leader, it is critical that you know where God is leading you. If you have no destination in mind as a leader, how could you possibly expect others to follow you? Ambition and drive will get you nowhere without a vision for how to achieve your goals.

Lack of vision (or distraction from a vision) can disqualify any leader. Scripture says that, "Where there is no vision, the people perish" (Prov. 29:18 KJV). Think, for a moment, about what's at stake in your leadership. You oversee a number of people in a business, home, congregation, etc. If you don't cast vision and guide correctly, you will adversely affect the many lives of those that follow you. However, if you cast vision and guide correctly, you could elevate many generations to come. That is what's at stake for you as a leader. If that doesn't both frighten and excite you, then leadership probably isn't for you. If it does, then let's proceed to the next section.

KNOW YOURSELF

The heart of a vision isn't the plan itself. It's the visionary behind the plan—the person God has created and the plan he has determined for his or her life. Before time began, God envisioned every moment of your life and the role you would play in his story here on earth. That God chose you to play a significant part in his story is an amazing thought! The more you understand who you are, the better you can use the skills, gifts and experiences God has given you to carry out his kingdom purposes.[1]

What leaders need more of today is emotional intelligence—"the ability to manage ourselves and our relationships effectively."[2] To be successful in leadership, leaders need to be aware of their story and how it has shaped them. When you understand your story, you begin to develop an emotional self-awareness that will greatly enhance your ability to self-assess, build your self-confidence and increase your self-control; this will, in turn, inform your ability to self-manage, increase social awareness and allow you to utilize your social skills in a beneficial way.[3]

My story began in Sherman, Texas, a small town sixty miles north of Dallas. I grew up in a single-parent household and, much like the biblical Timothy, I was raised by my mother and grandmother. God provided many people who would have significant influence in my life.

In many ways, I felt like "Milkman," the main character in Toni

Morrison's *Song of Solomon*, a novel about an African-American man on a quest to discover his cultural identity. As a child, I wanted to know about my heritage and where I came from just like "Milkman."

> A VISION IS WORTHLESS WITHOUT THE COURAGE TO WORK TOWARDS IT IN THE FACE OF GREAT OBSTACLES AND DIFFICULTIES THAT ARE SURE TO COME YOUR WAY.

The story of my ancestors was one marked by extraordinary struggle and oppression. They were slaves in the American South and were seen by many as merely property to be bought and sold for capital gain. They lacked the rights and privileges of an American citizen. This was the harsh reality my descendants lived in every day. However, behind this story of oppression is the strength and courage my ancestors possessed to pursue change and equality for black people. Their vision for a better tomorrow would change the course of our country and serve as a reminder that every story of pain and suffering can be redeemed for greater purposes. Without pain and suffering, we can never truly know how strong we are.

As I grew older, I began to discover more about my family's history. My family, like many families, didn't like to talk about the past, especially the ugly side of it. But I was compelled to know where I came from and set out on my own quest of discovery. What I found on that quest would reveal the richness of my heritage and how much of it shaped me into the man I am today.

My grandfather's family is from Charleston, South Carolina. It would not be an overstatement to say that Charleston was the epicenter of the American Slave Trade. Nearly one-third of the nation's slaves came through Charleston's trade market where they were auctioned off to the highest bidder on the city's riverfront.

My grandfather served in World War II and returned home to Charleston where he was shot to death for allegedly evading arrest. My family's recollection of the events surrounding his death suggest something entirely different. They contend he was killed for whistling at a white woman. Although he died in the '40s, his death was never openly discussed in my family for another fifty years.

My grandmother was left a widow responsible to provide for and raise three small children. She wasn't even thirty years old. But my grandmother was resilient. Instead of feeling sorry for herself or blaming others, she decided to stand. She could have used her emotional pain as an excuse to give up, but she did what she knew was right, despite her difficult circumstances. What she modeled in life remains an enduring character study in perseverance for my family and me.

Not long after my grandfather's death, our family would find itself in the middle of one of the biggest turning points in the Civil Rights Movement. One of our close relatives was Nathaniel Briggs, Jr., the petitioner in the *Briggs v. Elliot* case in Clarendon County. That case would pave the way for the historic *Brown v. Board of Education* case, which overturned racial segregation in the United States public school system. Life is interesting, isn't it? Race was an issue that had caused my family so much grief and pain, but it would also provide a platform to shift our country's attitudes and laws regarding African Americans.

It's hard for me to imagine the emotional weight my family members experienced under segregation in the Deep South. They endured death threats and public humiliation on a daily basis. What's more, many who were fighting for this cause abandoned them, because they felt like it was just too risky. The giant of racism was menacing and fierce. However, my descendants were determined to fulfill the mission set before them. Billy Holliday's song 'Strange Fruit' gives a great description of the temperature of that time: "Southern trees bear strange fruit / Blood on the leaves and blood at the root / Black bodies swinging in the southern breeze / Strange fruit hanging on the poplar trees." African Americans today are indebted to those that came before them who decided to risk their lives and stand, despite the odds and opposition before them.

WITHOUT PAIN AND SUFFERING, WE CAN NEVER TRULY KNOW HOW STRONG WE ARE.

When you look at your past, you'll find ugly places too. There'll be events and relationships you'd rather not revisit. Maybe your family is like mine, where the ugliness of your family's past is not talked about or even mentioned. If it is, you can be sure there are hurts and wounds among family members that have not healed. Perhaps you've found solace in running from your past and refusing to let it define who you are today. I would contend that's not the right way to find healing. Rather than running from the pain of your past, you can face the pain and find the keys to unlock strength and courage in your leadership. You need to be comfortable in your own skin and see that your past—the good and the bad—has shaped you to think, act and react in a certain way. When you understand that, you can leverage your past to help you to stand in the midst of any conflict.

I didn't find out about my ancestors' strength and courage to stand in the face of hate and cruelty until after the battle that's chronicled in this book. Looking back, I see that the internal compass within me that would not choose the road of convenience and safety was something I had inherited. Not running away and doing what I knew to be right was something that was built into me. While facing my own fight in ministry, that thing inside me said, "Never give up, no matter the cost to you. Do what's right and stand."

WINNING IS IN YOUR DNA

Each of us is composed of DNA, the hereditary material that carries genetic information and defines much of who are as human beings. Our DNA gives us the distinctive qualities and composition to make us who we are. God has created every person with a particular DNA structure and does this with a purpose in mind. I call it spiritual DNA. Each of us, with our unique personality, history and other traits, was designed to win in life.

If you were to look at my family's history, you'd think slaying giants was built into our DNA. My ancestors could have played the victim and been angry and bitter about their lot in life (something that causes us to lose focus on a vision in the midst of a fight), but they chose another path. They used their struggles to motivate them toward a goal:

to balance the scales of justice and win freedom and equality for their people. God has a plan for every crisis you face and I am convinced that he has given you what you need to see victory in those battles. The key to winning is staying attuned to his voice and seeing the story through to its completion.

Scripture tells us that whatever God has determined in your life, he will see it to completion (Phil. 1:6). Upon the blank pages of history God wrote your story with a special plan in mind. He created you for a successful life centered on him and his purposes. While we all want success in life, we are also reluctant to accept the unpredictability and difficulty that comes with it. We encounter plenty of struggle, pain, discomfort and conflict in our journey. But be encouraged. God is aware of the difficulties and experiences we face and has given each of us the right DNA to stand in the face of whatever comes along.

EACH OF US, WITH OUR UNIQUE PERSONALITY, HISTORY AND OTHER TRAITS, WAS DESIGNED TO WIN IN LIFE.

As an adult, I understand that where I came from contributed to what's in my DNA. My upbringing—with all of its influential characters and experiences—is the story that God has given me. Without the strong faith and character of my mother and grandmother, I would not be the man I am today. Without the experiences of facing giants as a child and young man, I would not have had the strength or the courage to stand and fight when my enemies attacked later on in adulthood.

While each of us takes our own path in life, we are all moving towards one goal as God's people—to fulfill his plan here on earth. In Matthew 16:19, Jesus tells his disciples that, by following him, they have been given authority to carry out their leadership calling: "I will give you the keys of the kingdom of heaven; whatever you bind on earth will be bound in heaven, and whatever you loose on earth will be loosed in heaven."

God has given you a specific assignment in his grand story. Everything about you—your past, present and future—has been ordained by God to make you the leader he purposed you to be. It's a fixed fight and God has preprogrammed you to win in the end. But, first, you must know who you are and *whose* you are. How we see ourselves matters.

Who we see ourselves to be is a result of the collective experiences and encounters in life that have shaped our thinking and perspective. If you think you're a failure, chances are there was a defining moment or experience that caused you to see yourself (and the world) through the lens of failure. The same can be said of those that see themselves as a winner.

The decisions we make in life form our patterns of response. We respond to life's circumstances in a particular way, because that's how we learned how to respond. People in our lives and events we faced taught us something about how the world works and the place we have in it. Often, our understanding of the world and ourselves is off-kilter and lacks right perspective. The good news is that we are not destined to repeat the failures and poor choices of the past. We can choose to break the cycle of repeating the past by drawing from our strengths, confronting our weaknesses and growing in character. In doing so, we will leave a legacy that others will want to follow.

MAKE SURE YOU ARE IN THE RIGHT PLACE

Once you discover who you are and the resources God has given you, make sure you are in the right place to carry out your vision. A good vision for the wrong place doesn't do much good; on the other hand, a good vision for the right place has enormous potential. I am certain that, if God entrusts you with a vision, he will put you in the right place to carry it out. Remember: he is directing your story towards fulfilling his purposes for your life and has given you everything you need to achieve great things for him.

When I was younger, being a pastor was not on my radar. It was a career that lacked professional prominence and prestige as far as I was concerned. I thought, "Who in their right mind would spend years in school and specialized training only to come out on the other end with debt and a job that didn't pay that well?" I wanted prominence and prestige. So I set my sights on practicing law instead of going into ministry.

Trust me when I tell you that pursuing the wrong things in life can cost you valuable time and money. If you're not fully convinced of that truth, just ask Jonah. Things didn't turn out so well for him. He heard God's call and ran from it. With that in mind, I thought I'd bargain with God by pursuing a joint degree in theology *and* law. I thought it was a win-win, because I would be obedient to his calling and gain the professional prestige I desired at the same time.

For a while my plan seemed to be working. However, that didn't mean that I was being obedient or successful in life. Getting what we want is not a recipe for success; it may appear that way for a season, but, unless you're following God's lead, your efforts will not have a lasting impact.

Thankfully, God never gave up on me and made sure I would pursue his calling on my life. His plans would eventually overrule mine and the day finally came when I surrendered my pursuit of prominence for a life in ministry. A week later I was connected to The Luke, the place God had chosen for me. It's remarkable how many opportunities arise when you simply obey God's calling. God had a plan for my life and wanted me in the pulpit. Looking back, I see that coming to The Luke would be a prelude to making a significant impact in the lives of others.

I wasn't aware of the church's past or any potential for future conflict when I interviewed to be the pastor. I was too young and naïve to ask those types of questions. Perhaps God was graciously withholding that information. Sometimes God will withhold valuable information from us to make sure we follow through with his purposes. Otherwise, we might pursue the well-traveled, comfortable route of what's safe and convenient.

The Luke was not located in a metropolitan area. Nor was it in a community that was thriving by any stretch of the imagination. The church didn't have the most attractive facility either. However, I knew this was where God wanted me. Those early days taught me not to be

> SOMETIMES GOD WILL WITHHOLD VALUABLE INFORMATION FROM US TO MAKE SURE WE FOLLOW THROUGH WITH HIS PURPOSES.

discouraged by what you find when you arrive at the destination God gives you. There's always more than what you see at first blush.

On the surface, The Luke was a small, community church. However, beneath the surface, God had a big vision for growth there. That vision included the church being led out of its quiet existence and into new, unfamiliar territory. As a leader, I was discovering that he led me to this specific purpose and had equipped me to carry it out. The vision wasn't just for me, but for all of the members. I knew that what I did as their leader then would have an effect on future generations.

My first sermon at the church was entitled "Authentic Power." The point I wanted to drive home in the sermon was that we receive real power when we are clear about who is in control of our lives, who is navigating our destiny and to whom we are called to submit. Only when we surrender to God's authentic power do we arrive at the destination that God has planned for us.

ASSESS YOUR CONTEXT

As a leader, it's important to know the context of the organization and its people you are leading. Do the necessary work up front to familiarize yourself with an organization's history and where it does business or ministry. Study demographic data within and beyond your organization to understand the wants, needs and desires of those you lead and those you hope to impact. Many leaders fail to do this and end up casting a misguided vision because of it. They forget to assess their context and discover who the vision is for and why it exists.

Of course, demographic research and data can only get you so far. Leaders need to get out among the people and engage them in conversation. Great leaders are great communicators. One key to excellent communication is mastering the art of listening and giving others enough space to tell their story. Given enough time, people will open up to you if you show them you're willing to listen. It's incredible what you can discover by asking the right questions and simply listening.

During my interview process with The Luke, I was asked to speak with the search committee at a local hotel. I sat in the middle of a long, executive table in a conference room. Each member of the committee came into the meeting with a folder full of background information on me. I could not have been more nervous. Throughout the entire meeting I was sweating through my shirt. I felt like I was testifying before a Congressional hearing!

One by one, they began asking questions like, "What is your view on the Trinity?" "What qualifies you to be a pastor?" "What is your view on women in ministry?" One of the members who had been fairly quiet asked me a question that has stuck with me to this day. Before asking his question, he mentioned my educational background and ministry accomplishments. Then, without missing a beat, he asked me, "Do you really think you can pastor us? We're just a small, country church."

His question told me something about the context of the church and how they viewed themselves. Without hesitation, I responded by saying, "No disrespect, but small, country church is a mentality, not an identity. I see God as much bigger than a small country church mentality." The room was silent. Slowly, smiles began to appear on the faces of those committee members.

They agreed with me, but they also knew the church had refused to explore greater possibilities in ministry. In the past, whenever the church experienced growth, there were those who fought to keep the church from expanding. They didn't want to chart out into unknown waters and preferred their small, manageable island of a congregation. They lacked confidence in a leader to take them places they had never been before.

If you want to thrive in leadership, those who follow you must have confidence in your leadership and vision. In short, they need to trust you in taking them to better and greater places.

God had called me to lead this church and I would not be satisfied with the status quo, because that's not in the character of God. Our God is big and doesn't intend for us to stay where we are. God never intended for anyone to be content with being small. No. He has much larger and greater plans for his people! The members of the search committee were genuinely seeking the will of God for the church. So was I. How we actually accomplished that would forever change the context of The Luke.

GET CLARITY ON THE VISION

Having a specific vision is essential. Often, we make the mistake of casting a vision that's too general. Vision casting isn't one-size-fits-all. It must be specific to your context. Otherwise, it is bound to derail, because you failed to take into consideration your context and personal gifts. In the end, it will leave those who follow you unsatisfied and unchanged.

The vision for our church hasn't changed since I became pastor. Our vision statement is simple: *Building bridges for future generations.* The way we accomplish building bridges is through our mission statement: *We are a community of bridge-builders who seek to worship and celebrate God's active presence in our lives and engage in transformative ministry to the whole person through spiritual development, social witness, economic empowerment and health awareness.*

When I accepted the call to pastor, I was confident in the vision God had for our church, but I needed specificity on how it applied to our particular context. While the vision hasn't changed, its application is always changing and evolving as our cultural context changes as well.

The simple truth is that it's easier for people to follow you when they know where you are taking them. The responsibility is on you, the leader, to craft a clear vision. If you want to test your effectiveness in this area, just ask one of your employees (or congregants) to state the organization's vision in one sentence. If they can't, your vision probably needs work.

CAST THE VISION

Once you have a clear vision, you have to communicate it. As a leader, you're primarily responsible for casting vision in such a way that others catch it. Habakkuk, one of the Minor Prophets in the Old Testament, was charged to "write the vision and make it plain" (Hab. 2:2). God wanted his message to be crystal clear and didn't want to leave any room for confusion or misunderstanding. Likewise, you have been charged with communicating a vision so clearly that even the most casual observer understands the identity and purpose of your organization or ministry.

In casting the vision, be as specific as possible. Don't use words or concepts that are too generic. Instead, be specific about what you are called to accomplish. You can't achieve a goal without being clear on what the goal is. Those who follow you will eventually burn out and drop off for lack of a clearly communicated vision.

If outreach is your vision, then tell people how and to whom you are going to reach out. If creating wealth and developing a financially strong organizational climate is your vision, then tell those you lead how those things are going to happen. If creating a stronger family life is your vision, tell family members what you have to do to make that a reality. Great leaders are specific about what they are called to do. That way everyone can find his or her place in the vision.

Any visitor to The Luke should know by the time they leave one of our services that we are building bridges for future generations. It's something we incorporate into every aspect of our ministry. We make a point to say it throughout our services, especially when welcoming visitors. Not only do we say it, we also demonstrate it in how we engage our members and communities. In any given service, multiple generations of believers gather for our worship experience. It's truly inspiring to look out and see teenagers, young families and seniors all worshiping as one body.

You must be committed to and consistent in casting vision. A lot of people will get behind a vision at first. However, in time, there is the tendency for people to splinter off when things get tough or change is slow. As a leader, you model consistency and what it looks like to commit to something and see it through to its completion.

Keeping the focus of a group can be difficult, especially in challenging seasons. That's why it is important to keep the vision fresh in people's minds by repeating it often. I make a point to do this whenever I have the opportunity. Whether it's from the pulpit, at the park or over breakfast with a member, I want people to know why The Luke exists and what we're working to accomplish. And I encourage everyone to do the same.

People want a leader who is authentic. You must live out your vision and let it breathe in you. Your vision should be a lifestyle that people see in you day in and day out. Find ways to weave your vision into the different aspects of your leadership, whether that's from the stage, in conversations, on your website, etc. If you're consistent in living out your vision, it won't be long before people start living it out with you. Ultimately, you want the vision to be something contagious that spreads beyond your organization to others.

Casting vision does take time and requires a degree of patience and persistence in the process. In my case, it took almost a decade for our leadership and congregation to catch the vision. We made sure our vision was communicated clearly in every meeting, training session and church publication for years on end. In time people started to catch it and that's when things really started to take off.

In short, a good vision is meaningless if it's not communicated clearly. If you cast the vision and commit to it long-term, people will take notice. They'll see a dedicated, consistent leader who will ride the storms of conflict out and not be deterred by challenges and opposition.

As a leader, God has called you to carry out his vision. Remember your story and consider how God has used it to prepare you to be the kind of leader that will stand in the face of giants and keep others from majoring on minor things. If you allow him to navigate your path, he will help you fulfill the vision he has given you.

In between casting your vision and fulfilling your vision, you must overcome conflicts. To successfully lead others through conflict, you need to define the conflict. How can you fight the good fight (and win) if you don't know who or what you're fighting?

DISCUSSION QUESTIONS

1. What are the events, relationships and skills God has given you in your spiritual DNA? How do these help you to be a more effective leader?

2. Has God given you a vision for your area of leadership? If so, what is it? If not, what steps can you take to receive that vision?

3. Are you ready to cast your vision? If so, what steps are you taking to cast it? If not, what is hindering you?

4. How will you live out your vision for those who are following you?

3

DEFINE THE CONFLICT

*The more we run from conflict, the more it masters us; the more we try
to avoid it, the more it controls us; the less we fear conflict, the less it
confuses us; the less we deny our differences, the less they divide us.*

DAVID AUGSBURGER

What words come to your mind when you heard the word *conflict*? For some, the term denotes a long-lasting disagreement or argument between two people or groups that is characterized by antagonism or hostility. Others may see it in terms of an armed struggled between two opposing forces. A third group might view conflict as incompatibility between two or more opinions, principles or interests.

While all of these are correct, I want to draw your attention to something common in each definition: the threat conflict poses. Conflict will occur naturally between two people or groups that share different opinions and personalities.[1] However, when conflict goes beyond those differences and persists over time, we will eventually sense that our personal or professional well-being (i.e., comfort, health, happiness) is being threatened in some way.[2] Sometimes the perceived threat is legitimate; other times it is not. Skilled leaders are able to discern between the legitimate and illegitimate threats and respond appropriately to the conflict at hand.

Think about a significant conflict you've encountered in the last three months. I would venture to say you could pinpoint some threat you felt in that conflict. Maybe it was your reputation at work. Perhaps it was your authority as a leader. Whatever the situation, you were given two choices in the conflict: retreat or respond. From an early age, many of us were taught to retreat and avoid conflict because it was too risky, awkward, emotionally draining or frustrating. Few were taught to face the conflict and respond in a quick and constructive way. In this chapter we'll discuss how to respond—rather than retreat—when we encounter conflict.

START WITH THE END IN MIND

In Chapter Two I highlighted the importance of having a clear and compelling vision as a leader. Having vision helps us when we encounter conflict along the path toward fulfilling God's call. Great leaders begin with a vision and use it to maneuver through difficulty on the way to seeing it fulfilled. The leaders we remember are the ones that saw beyond the present (how things are) and into the future (how things could be).

Nelson Mandela was such a leader. Like Joseph in the Bible, he spent much of his life waiting to see his vision come to fruition. Mandela was imprisoned for nearly thirty years in a South African jail before being released. Four years after his release, he became the first democratically elected president of South Africa. He was seventy-five years old. Despite long years in the wilderness, Mandela's vision for national reconciliation in his country compelled him to carry on. His vision for a better tomorrow helped him stay the course and endure present hardships in prison. It took a lifetime to fulfill, but Mandela entered a

"Promised Land" experience, because he refused to give up on what he believed South Africans were capable of achieving.

No doubt Mandela pondered many things while confined to his small cell all those years. If ever a man was empowered by a vision, it was Mandela. He wasn't focused on the conflict and hardship at hand. Rather, he was focused on the end result. It gave him hope that tomorrow was filled with possibilities beyond his imagination. As president, he became a major player in moving South Africa—a country marked by racial discrimination—towards greater harmony and understanding. Leaders like Mandela remind us of the importance of looking past the conflict to see the end result.

CONFLICT IS NORMAL AND NECESSARY

Here's the simple truth: people are different and that means we won't always agree. How boring and colorless would life be if we all thought alike? What if we all listened to the same music, vacationed at the same destinations and ate the same food? Our different perspectives fill this world with color and intrigue. No two people are alike and that's a great thing! Because we're different, sooner or later we are going to disagree with someone about something. This is especially true within the dynamics of a team or organization.

It takes a multiplicity of people and personalities to make an organization function well. A whole arsenal of skills and gifts need to be utilized to bring a big vision to fulfillment. Great leaders have the ability to leverage different personalities and gifts in a productive way. And great leaders understand that conflict among such a dynamic group is inevitable.

Let's go ahead and accept the fact that things never go entirely as planned. Even the best strategies are subject to change. Too many variables are at play with people and circumstances to think we could do everything exactly as we had envisioned. A four-star general's battle plans always change once the bullets start flying. A football coach will never execute his game plan without some in-game adjustments.

Conflict is natural within an organization.[3] Often, it's the result of moving a number of people with different perspectives in the same direction. Conflict can also be an incredible catalyst for innovation and creativity.[4] Therefore, don't immediately think that when you encounter conflict you've done something wrong as a leader. You may very well be doing exactly what you're supposed to do. Conflict is a byproduct of change. People can quickly become comfortable with doing things a certain way and resist anything that alters their program. The desire for comfort can easily lead to complacency and resistance to change. Complacency can stunt an organization and keep it from flourishing. The axiom that, *if you do things the way you always have, you will keep getting what you've always gotten*, speaks to the dangers of complacency in an organization. I would go so far as to say that any organization unwilling to change will eventually fail and be forgotten.

> CONFLICT CAN ALSO BE AN INCREDIBLE CATALYST FOR INNOVATION AND CREATIVITY.

I thought everyone would embrace my vision for change at The Luke with open arms. While I was asking the church to make a major change, I thought the vision was compelling enough to get everyone on board. Boy, was I wrong! Those resistant to change were compliant with my leadership as long as I didn't rock the boat. As soon as I started rocking it with change, conflict came knocking.

I have never experienced major change in an organization without some conflict. Change is rarely easy and leaders should expect conflict when they challenge the status quo. So don't be surprised when you encounter it. Change is part of the process of moving a vision towards reality. As a leader, your job is to guide others through the change and address conflict in a constructive way that propels your people (and vision) forward.

The good news is that conflict could be a sign that you are headed in the right direction. When I look at great leaders from the past, I see every one of them facing conflict on some scale. Often, that conflict came from those that directly opposed those leaders—and the changes they pursued. Winston Churchill once said, "a kite flies against the wind, not with it." As a leader, you need to understand that you will be going into the wind much of the time. Often, you will have the winds of support from others behind you. Other times you won't. The most important thing to understand is that, no matter what your circumstance, God gives you flight as a leader. It's not about you. It's about him and his glory. Find your confidence in him and his calling. When that happens, conflict will look more like a stepping-stone than a roadblock.

You need a keen idea of where you are leading others and what resources (internal and external) you have at your disposal to fulfill your purposes. This requires an examination of your own heart as a leader. What purpose do you serve as a leader? Do the right things motivate you? Are you focused on the main things? Is anything keeping you from flourishing as a leader?

DETERMINE THE REAL ISSUES

Some of you reading this can easily identify conflicts you're currently facing as a leader. What you'd like are ways to actually deal with it. Well, there are a number of things you can do to equip yourself to maneuver through conflict in a healthy and helpful way; they will also sharpen your vision and help you understand your role in it.

First, gather information. The biggest step you can take in dealing with conflict is to know what you need to know in order to properly assess a situation. If you came into an organization, consider its background (e.g., history, people, reputation, etc.). Understanding the context of a conflict will give you clues to identify the real issue(s) at hand.

Early in my pastorate, I was told a story that played a major role in shaping what The Luke had become. The church was founded in 1900. For decades, the church blended well in the small community of Humble, Texas. However, in the 1930's the decision was made to make the city an all-white community. Church members were told they had to uproot and move across the tracks to an area know as "Bordersville."

Knowing this provided me clues as to why some members opposed moving the church. On the surface, it appeared that the opposition was against the growth and success of the church. Upon closer inspection, however, I found that this change felt like history repeating itself to them. They were being pushed out and asked to leave what had become the church's home for many years. Old wounds were reopened and a spirit of bitterness began to spread among some of the members.

Along with this issue, I noticed another one. Over the church's 100-year history, they had hired fifteen pastors. About every seven years, the church would have to adjust to new leadership. The continual departure of pastors left the church with a lot of pain and lack of trust. Many of the members were cynical about change in leadership and looked at the latest pastor as simply the next one up to bat. Many were leery of me when I became pastor, because they had been let down and hurt before I arrived.

Knowing the church's background helped me walk the church through a necessary healing process. Pinpointing the real issues at work in the church gave me a clearer picture of the conflict I was facing there. I was able to understand my opposition and why they felt the way they did. Their opposition was rooted more in their pain than in my vision for the church. I would not have understood that without first knowing where they had come from and what they had experienced.

DON'T TAKE IT PERSONALLY

One of the best lessons I've learned in leadership is not to take conflict personally. It's easy to feel as if conflict in your leadership is a personal affront to you—as if people have put a target on your back and are aiming for it. It was only after I learned about The Luke's history that I began to understand that it was not about me as their leader. I discovered past hurts, disappointments and discouragements that were holding some members back. They didn't want to move forward, because they thought it too painful. The sooner I learned this, the sooner we could all move forward. I needed the bigger picture to see that it wasn't about me and that this move was God's vision for the church. I see now that God not only wanted to see his name glorified in his vision being fulfilled, but was also concerned with *how* it was carried out.

When we take conflict personally, it will cost us. It may cost us time, money, health, relationships or energy. Overall, it will hinder your leadership and keep you from fulfilling your vision. When people oppose you, they often project their own hurts, hang-ups and insecurities on to you. It's a reflection of their own reality and has little to do with you. Every situation is not a personal attack. Therefore, take the time to listen to others and get their perspective. Learn who your opposition is and where they've come from, and make room for God to help you in the process.

CONFLICT CAN HELP YOU FIND YOUR HARMONIOUS SYNERGY

Many view conflict in a negative light without exception. The truth is, conflict can bring out the best qualities in you and those who follow you. You may even find that conflict can unify a group in a powerful way.

A good example of this is Arthur Schopenhauer's *Porcupine Parable*. The story goes that, on a cold day, a group of porcupines huddled together for warmth; but when they felt the pain of one another's quills, they quickly moved apart. When they felt the cold again, they moved close together. However, as before, the stab of their quills caused them to move apart. Over and over again, the porcupines moved back and forth—together and apart—until they finally found the right distance that would give them the warmth they needed but without feeling the pain of one another's quills.

We are not unlike the porcupines in Schopenhauer's parable. In isolation, we experience loneliness and emptiness, which amplifies our desire for community. However, when we come together, our individual faults and issues are exposed and cause conflict, driving us apart. The key to living in the warmth of community is to find the optimal distance where people can co-exist without being too far apart (no relationship) or too close (relationship without boundaries) to one another. Community can be messy and complicated. Therefore, boundaries are necessary to have relational balance and intimacy that doesn't isolate or suffocate. And, like the porcupines in Schopenhauer's parable, it takes the entire community to achieve that balance.

Leaders need to pursue what I call a "harmonious synergy" within community—utilizing the different opinions and perspectives of those in your organization to fulfill a common purpose. Instead of allowing conflict to drive people in your organization further apart, seek out ways to unify others and move your vision forward. The porcupines' conflict (stabbing each other with their quills) caused them to work together to find a solution that benefited everyone involved. The same outcome can be achieved in your organization if you model a harmonious synergy that encourages everyone to work together to find a solution to conflicts that arise.[5]

While we, as leaders, encourage everyone to work together to resolve conflicts, we understand that there will be those who don't go along with the program. There are the obstinate few out there who, despite your efforts to persuade, refuse to cooperate with the group. It seems that they are resolved never to change their opinions or course of action. This is unfortunate, but should not come as a shock.

A sure sign that your leadership needs reassessment is when you *don't* experience resistance. It could mean that you're running in the same direction as the opposition! Of course, you shouldn't go out there looking to make enemies. But, if you're working to achieve a God-given vision, you can expect to run into opposing forces along the way.

Someone who ran into serious opposition in fulfilling a vision was Nehemiah. He shows up on the pages of Scripture during the Persian Empire, which replaced Babylon as the greatest power in the ancient Near East. Nearly a century earlier, the Babylonians conquered Jerusalem and led the Israelites into exile. In 538 B.C., Cyrus, king of Persia, issued a decree that allowed the Israelites to return to their homeland.

Under Sheshbazzar and Ezra's leadership, the Jews returned to Jerusalem and rebuilt the temple in the years that followed. In 445 B.C., Nehemiah, the cupbearer for King Artaxerxes, heard that the returning Jews were in trouble and that Jerusalem's walls had been torn down. Nehemiah, who had found favor with King Artaxerxes, was given leave (along with everything he needed) to go to Jerusalem and help the Israelites rebuild the wall.

Although Nehemiah's mission would serve the good of his

countrymen, he met opposition from those in neighboring cities. The threat of the opposition was so great that Nehemiah and the rest of the Israelites were on constant alert; they had to be prepared for battle at all times. Therefore, they worked on rebuilding the wall with a sword in one hand and a trowel in the other. Despite the opposition, Nehemiah kept his followers focused on achieving what he was sent to Jerusalem to accomplish.

Although it can be unpleasant, conflict has a way of building up your leadership muscles. Like an athlete or soldier, you have to develop those muscles with daily exercise and training. Conflict is the workout you need to strengthen those muscles! Without it, things like conformity (lack of creativity and innovation) and mediocrity (having a low standard of excellence) will cause those leadership muscles to atrophy. As John F. Kennedy once said, "Conformity is the jailer of freedom and the enemy of growth." Remind yourself and those who follow you to expect conflict and opposition on the road towards change. When you expect it, you can prepare for it and know how to stand when conflict comes your way.

When you're pursuing God's vision and feel the heat from your opposition, see it as God's assurance that you're headed in the right direction. As the fight intensified in my story, I had to learn how to use the conflict to lead others. I took it as an opportunity to prepare others for the fight by showing them the potential for growth in conflict. With God's directing, the conflict ended up making us a stronger vessel for his work.

LOOK AT THE CONFLICT FROM DIFFERENT ANGLES

Sometimes we can get caught in the fog of a conflict and lose our vision. Therefore, it's important to not lose focus and know how to respond well in the midst of conflict. In law school we were taught to study a case from as many angles as possible, taking into consideration every side of the story. We should do the same in conflict, because our view is not the only one. Take an investigative approach in handling on-going conflict by seeing it from every possible angle.

Before undertaking his project, Nehemiah took a night journey to Jerusalem to inspect the city's walls and assess the damage (Neh. 2:9-20). Nehemiah had to take into account how much damage was done and what he would need (i.e., time, resources, labor) to complete the project. As a leader, you have an obligation to study the conflict in order to develop a solution that addresses the existing problem and benefits everyone involved.

Keep in mind that your perspective in a given conflict is not the only one. I learned that by having to lead in a situation where my church's members were still dealing with unresolved pain and bitterness that had become part of the church's culture. A small group had gained influence and was hindering the church's growth and progress under the guise of "maintaining the historical integrity of the church." In the past, when a pastor went against this group, he was quickly confronted and fired. And for years that response kept things at The Luke moving along without major changes.

If you want to win the fight, you must understand the perspective of your opponent. My job was to lead an entire congregation, including those that opposed me in my vision to expand the church. God had called me to stay true to his vision for the church. But I also needed to pursue a diplomatic solution that would restore the church and quell the dissention. In order to do that, I had to understand the pain behind the opposition. Once I did that, I could seek the best possible resolution for everyone.

Conflict is inevitable, but you have choices in how to deal with it. Your organization doesn't have to just survive in conflict; you can thrive in it if you see it as opportunity for growth and progress. Conflict will show you what you are made of and where you need to be strengthened as a leader and organization.

The journey towards fulfilling your vision is long and often hard. As you traverse the conflicts and difficulties of leadership, it's important to have the right guidance. Thankfully, you already have a wealth of wisdom at your disposal to give you the right direction and motivation to press on in your journey.

DISCUSSION QUESTIONS

1. When facing conflict, how do you identify surface tensions and the underlying issues beneath them?

2. What are the possible consequences of taking conflict personally in leadership? What steps can you take to avoid taking conflict personally?

3. What would it look like for you, as a leader, to create harmonious synergy (utilizing the different opinions and perspectives of those in your organization to fulfill a common purpose) while addressing conflict) in your organization?

4. Why is it important to understand the perspective of those that oppose you? How do you go about gaining that perspective as a leader?

4

SEEK THE RIGHT GUIDANCE

Leadership and learning are indispensable to each other.

JOHN F. KENNEDY

In the Bible, many men and women have been driven to seek the Lord in the midst of conflict. Proverbs 28:2 says, "When the country is in chaos, everybody has a plan to fix it—but it takes a leader of real understanding to straighten things out" (The Message). In dealing with conflict, sooner or later we all come to the realization that we don't have all the answers. No one does. We are simply too limited in our understanding and experience to know exactly what to do in every situation. That's why we need wisdom and direction from others who have traveled the path before us.

It's easy to be enveloped by the intensity of conflict when we're in middle of it. Conflict presents a crisis and, within a crisis, it's tempting to expend all our resources in an attempt to bring resolution. It takes mature leadership to admit your limitations and seek the assistance of those experienced in handling the unique challenges every conflict presents.

Jehoshaphat was a leader who wasn't afraid to seek guidance in conflict. With his enemies readying for war against Judah, he went to the Lord in prayer and called for a national fast. Scripture tells us all of Judah knelt before the Lord and prayed for deliverance. God answered his people and gave guidance through divine directives. His reply was simply that the battle was not theirs to win. It was his and he would deliver them and give them victory.

Like Jehoshaphat, I learned the importance of seeking the right guidance in life. For many of us, we can point to one or more influential mentors that invested in us and showed us what it looked like to live in the light of God's wisdom. In doing so, they showed how dependent they were on God and others for guidance; they couldn't do it on their own and didn't expect us to either.

No man is an island. You need a support circle to help you as a leader. You need people to speak truth in your life; to expose your blind spots; to tell you what you need to hear and not necessarily what you want to hear. You need someone in your corner who will encourage you to stay in the fight when it becomes intense. You need supporters who'll stand with you in the rough-and-tumble world of leadership.

Early in my leadership, there were times in conflict when I spent more time hiding from it rather than seeking help from others. I misjudged people and drew false conclusions. Like all leaders, I'm human, which means I sometimes perceive things incorrectly and make mistakes. That being said, I've come to discover that successful leaders know how to be humble and seek assistance. They don't let pride or ego get in the way of them getting the help they need. In my story, I was surprised by the amount of people willing to offer their support and stand with me in the heat of battle.

CONSULT DIVINE GUIDANCE FIRST

Jehoshaphat did the best thing a leader can do when faced with conflict: he went to the Source of all wisdom for a battle strategy. He whisked right past the counsel of men, went to the temple, got on his knees and petitioned the Lord for divine assistance. Jehoshaphat modeled for us the importance of getting a higher perspective on how to handle conflict. God doesn't expect you to fight your battles on your own strength and wisdom. God answers those that diligently seek his face. "I sought the Lord and he answered me; he delivered me from all my fears" (Psalm 34:4).

In Jehoshaphat's prayer, he recalled the history of Israel and how God had delivered them from their enemies. His vulnerability in the prayer is truly humbling; he didn't hold anything back from God about the desperate situation Israel found itself in.

Proverbs 3:5-6 says, "Trust in the Lord with all your heart and lean not on your own understanding; in all your ways submit to him, and he will make your paths straight." If we want God's guidance, we must first submit to him. Otherwise, we'll try to fit God into our plans and strategies. Trusting God means that we acknowledge his wisdom above our own and lean upon him for understanding. Only then will he make our paths straight. Whether God speaks to you directly or through another person or circumstance, you can be assured that seeking God first pays major dividends.

BE BOLD BUT HONEST

Take Jehoshaphat's cue and be honest when you seek direction in leadership. Don't be afraid to admit where you've fallen short as a leader and that you don't know how to handle a situation. God can handle your honesty. He already knows what you're going through and how you're feeling. And he is honored when we humble ourselves before him and reach out for help. Being transparent with the Almighty shows faith that he is able to give you wisdom and strength.

It is also important to be honest with those you're leading. It's far more effective to be open and honest about conflict than to conceal it. Of course, it's important to exercise discretion in sharing the conflict at the appropriate time. It's not an opportunity to air dirty laundry and single people out. Rather, it's your responsibility, as a leader, to inform those who follow you what an organization is going through and the steps its leadership is taking to resolve the conflict.

Early on, I was resolved not to involve The Luke's members in what was going on at the church. At the time, I felt like they were just too fragile. I was concerned that families and children might get caught in the crossfire of this conflict. As their leader, I knew I could handle the brunt of the blows for a time.

Then came the tipping point when I realized that, if I didn't open up about the conflict, the church's members wouldn't be able to stand in faith. In fact, I was robbing them of the opportunity to stand. How could I expect them to grow and mature as believers if I kept them unaware of what God was doing at the church? I wanted to protect them from further pain, but I was impeding their growth. If we were to grow as a community, I needed to be honest with them and shine a light on the situation. My motivation was that doing this would keep rumors from spreading and turning into dissention, which could split the church and cause further damage.

LEADERS NEED A SAFE PLACE TO EXPRESS THEIR EMOTIONS AND STRUGGLES.

Being honest with others takes away one of the enemy's greatest weapons: circulating secrets and lies in the dark. Great leaders aren't afraid of the dark. They pull the covers off it and expose it to the light. We must be open and honest with one another if we hope to keep conflict from turning destructive and causing collateral damage in our organizations. Remember: you are responsible for those who follow you. Allowing conflict to fester will, ultimately, cause them further pain and loss.

Leaders need a safe place to express their emotions and struggles. Find someone with whom you can be transparent. It can be a trusted friend, pastor or counselor—anyone that is qualified and experienced in dealing with conflict as a leader. Far too many leaders feel as if they have to struggle alone. With everyone looking to them for guidance, they can't bear the thought of admitting that they need guidance themselves. So they isolate themselves from others, make themselves busier at work or hide their real emotions with overconfidence, charisma, charm, etc.

If you're married, share what you're going through with your spouse. There's no excuse for not inviting your other half to walk with you through conflict. Give them the opportunity to stand with you. They can be strong for you when you cannot seem to find the strength yourself. And they can encourage and speak truth to you like no other, because they know you better than anyone. I was blessed through our church's conflict to have the greatest spouse and support that any leader could ask for. My wife was a model of strength and she continually prayed for me and stood with me every step of the way.

We need boldness when we're being honest before the Lord. Be bold and unashamed in your prayers. Paul tells us in Philippians 4:6 not to "be anxious about anything, but in every situation, by prayer and petition, with thanksgiving, present your requests to God." Prayer changes things. Plain and simple. Jehoshaphat believed that. That's why he called all of Judah to fast, pray and wait on God to respond.

Keep in constant communication with the Lord inside and outside of conflict. He is always at work to accomplish his purposes in your leadership and make you a better leader in the process. I began to realize that, by seeking the Lord and opening up about my internal struggle, I was experiencing greater spiritual intimacy with him. God was revealing more of himself to me and I was learning more about myself as well. My prayer life deepened and I was experiencing the sweetness of his Spirit in my daily devotional reading. Regularly communing with the Lord put me in a position to hear his voice when he answered my prayers. God didn't take me out of the battle, but he gave me the internal strength I needed to get through it.

God never said he would keep out you of conflict. On the contrary, he often puts us right in the middle of it. But take heart. You're not alone in the fight. You are there for a purpose and the Lord wants to make his name known in your situation. All he asks you to do is seek him and trust him. If you will keep your mind and heart focused on those two things, I am confident that God will give you everything you need to get through the most difficult circumstances.

DEVELOP A TEAM OF CONFIDANTS

Be sure that your support circle has integrity, is trustworthy and able to keep what you share in confidence. You need freedom to share all the details of your situation. That way, your team of confidants will have the necessary information they need to offer their perspectives and guidance. How do you determine if people have integrity? Watch them. See if what they say matches what they actually do. If the two line up, then they have integrity and are trustworthy.

In the beginning of my conflict, I struggled to seek help from my peers. Frankly, I thought this conflict would soon blow over and that everything would go back to normal. I thought I was David facing Goliath. It didn't take long for me to realize that I needed outside help; I couldn't get through this battle alone. Fortunately, God provided the right people at the right time to help me (and the rest of our leadership).

> CONSIDER THE EXISTING RESOURCES AND PEOPLE AVAILABLE TO YOU, AND BUILD A TEAM OF CONFIDANTS THAT WILL WALK WITH YOU THROUGH YOUR CONFLICT.

Consider the existing resources and people available to you, and build a team of confidants that will walk with you through your conflict. Proverbs 11:14 tells us that, "where there is no guidance, a people fall, but in an abundance of counselors there is safety." I cannot begin to express my gratitude for the men and women that stood by me, encouraged me and believed in the vision that I had for our church. Their faithfulness is a testimony to God's provision. I would not be the leader I am today without their trust and willingness to stand with me.

Sometimes God provides help from the most unsuspecting of places. During the time Moses was leading the Israelites through the wilderness, King Balak of Moab summoned Balaam, a sorcerer, to curse God's people. God visited Balaam and told him not to curse the Israelites. Balaam initially obeyed, but then decided to travel with a group of King Balak's people. On the way, Balaam's donkey saw the Angel of the

Lord standing in their path. Three times the donkey tried to turn away from the Angel, and, each time, Balaam beat the animal in response. After the third time, the Lord opened the donkey's mouth and said to Balaam, "What have I done to you to make you beat me these three times?" If God can use a donkey to get his point across, surely he can help you in a myriad of ways in the midst of your conflict.

LISTEN ATTENTIVELY AND ACT ACCORDINGLY

Listen to your team of confidants and be receptive to their counsel. Commit to following their counsel, provided it is consistent with Scripture. Consider their advice in terms of its relevance to your current situation. Also consider the moral, ethical and legal implications of their counsel. If you are uncertain about any advice you receive, ask for clarification or the opinion of other confidants. Ultimately, have your team go before the Lord in prayer regarding any and all advice received.

The truth is, not everyone will give you good advice despite the best of intentions. In my situation, I had a number of pastors who were watching everything unfold at The Luke. They told me to cut my losses, start fresh somewhere else and learn from the experience. In their eyes, there was too much at stake and they didn't want to see me consumed (or overtaken) by the fight. Their advice didn't sit well with me. I knew God had a vision for our church and that I wasn't called to throw in the towel because of this conflict. I viewed success as lining up with God's will, and leaving The Luke would be stepping outside of his will.

Now, it's one thing to listen to good advice. It's quite another to actually follow through and apply it. Faith always requires a response. James tells us that, "faith by itself, if it does not have works, is dead" (James 2:17). James also says, "Do not merely listen to the word, and so deceive yourself. Do what it says" (James 1:22). Great leaders will listen to good advice and act accordingly. If you receive good advice and do nothing, what does that say about how you truly feel about it? I would contend that you don't have much faith in it.

God gave Jehoshaphat a message through one of his priests, Jahaziel. He told the king, "This is what the Lord says to you: 'Do not be afraid or discouraged because of this vast army. For the battle is not yours, but God's'" (2 Chron. 20:15). That advice turned the tide of the battle in Judah's favor. Jahaziel went on to encourage God's people, reminding the king to stand firm and see the deliverance of the Lord. Judah's deliverance came when Jehoshaphat listened to Jahaziel's advice and responded in faith.

The right guidance can go a long way in helping you create a battle plan in leadership. No two conflicts are alike; each conflict presents its own unique set of challenges and possible solutions. If you want to lead others towards a vision fulfilled, you must take the time to strategize and develop a winning strategy for the fight.

DISCUSSION QUESTIONS

1. What are the dangers of leaders not being honest with others about conflict in their organization? What are benefits of being honest?

2. If you were to build a team of confidants, who would be on your team? What character traits do they have that qualify them?

3. What character traits would disqualify someone from being on your team?

4. How do you determine if someone's advice is good or bad?

5. What is the best advice you've received from someone about a conflict (or a challenging situation) you were facing?

5

CREATE A BATTLE PLAN

*In preparing for battle, I have always found that plans
are useless, but planning is indispensable.*

DWIGHT D. EISENHOWER

Military leaders will tell you preparation for battle matters just as much as much as what happens in the heat of a conflict. Before one shot is fired, weeks—if not months—of preparation go into training troops and developing a plan of attack. In the world of sports, championships are won by teams that have created a winning strategy by studying their opponent's strengths and weaknesses alongside their own.

Good looks and charisma will only get you so far in life. Being the type of leader that will stand in the midst of conflict is more than the white in your smile or the title on your door. Leadership is more than showing up and cheerleading others. Leadership requires long-term planning and the ability to move others forward to accomplish goals.

While things like intellect and networking ability are great attributes, intentionality in decision-making is the defining quality of great leaders.

As a journalist for a business magazine in the 1930s, Napoleon Hill studied the habits of over 500 millionaires, including Andrew Carnegie, Henry Ford and Charles M. Schwab. Through his investigative work he found one characteristic they all shared: decisiveness. In his book *Think and Grow Rich* (Capstone: 2011), Hill writes that, "analysis of several hundred people who had accumulated fortunes well beyond the million dollar mark disclosed the fact that *every one of them* had the habit of reaching decisions promptly."[1] For Hill, a decisive mindset was the characteristic that set this successful group apart from those that procrastinated and failed to act when necessary.

> GOD CALLED HIS PEOPLE TO LOOK TO HIM AS THEIR GENERAL AND OBEY HIS EVERY INSTRUCTION.

As a leader, Jehoshaphat faced the biggest decision in his reign as king. His enemies were marching towards Judah with intent to destroy the capital and take the nation captive. Imagine the fear Judah's enemies struck in the hearts of onlookers as their three-headed army went through neighboring cities on the way to Jerusalem. Each stomp and battle cry of the opposition would have made it clear that war was drawing closer. On the surface, Jehoshaphat was cooked. Judah was outnumbered and overmatched in every way. The nation was backed into a corner with nowhere to turn. Jehoshaphat had a God-sized problem that required a God-sized solution if he wanted to see another sunrise.

Throughout Israel's history God proved to be a master military strategist. He needed to be, because the Israelites rarely found themselves in a fight where they weren't the underdog. They were a small nation surrounded by superpowers like Egypt, Assyria, Babylon, Persia, Greece and Rome. God called his people to look to him as their General and obey his every instruction. Obedience and trust were required if Israel hoped to see victory on the battlefield.

At the beginning of the Book of Joshua, the Israelites, having spent forty years wandering in the wilderness, were preparing to enter the Promised Land. Although Canaan was promised to the Israelites, it would not simply be given to them; they would have to conquer its inhabitants, many of which were giants. As the Israelites were approaching the Jordan River, God gave Joshua, Israel's new leader, these instructions in 1:6-9:

> Be strong and courageous, for you shall cause this people to inherit the land that I swore to their fathers to give them. Only be strong and very courageous, being careful to do according to all the law that Moses my servant commanded you. Do not turn from it to the right hand or to the left, that you may have good success wherever you go. This Book of the Law shall not depart from your mouth, but you shall meditate on it day and night, so that you may be careful to do according to all that is written in it. For then you will make your way prosperous, and then you will have good success. Have I not commanded you? Be strong and courageous. Do not be frightened, and do not be dismayed, for the LORD your God is with you wherever you go.

God's message to Judah was essentially the same in 2 Chronicles 20:15-17:

> "Do not be afraid and do not be dismayed at this great horde, for the battle is not yours but God's. Tomorrow go down against them. Behold, they will come up by the ascent of Ziz. You will find them at the end of the valley, east of the wilderness of Jeruel. You will not need to fight in this battle. Stand firm, hold your position, and see the salvation of the LORD on your behalf, O Judah and Jerusalem. Do not be afraid and do not be dismayed. Tomorrow go out against them, and the LORD will be with you."

Judah was called to stand against their enemies and fight with the confidence that God would be with them. With God on their side, no army could defeat them.

One of my favorite battles in the Bible takes place after Israel entered the Promised Land when judges ruled over Israel. God called Gideon, Israel's fifth judge, to lead the Israelites against the Midianites. So Gideon assembled 32,000 men for battle. However, God said he had too many people and asked Gideon to pare down his army by asking those who were afraid to fight to return home—22,000 left, leaving Gideon with 10,000. Still, God still thought Gideon had too many men and asked him to pare them down even more. So Gideon took his soldiers down to the water to let them drink. God instructed him to take those that cupped the water with their hand to drink rather than those who got down on their knees to drink (Judg. 7:5-7). In the end, Gideon was left with only 300 men.

Gideon and his small army encamped at on the outskirts of the Midianite camp at night. Gideon didn't arm his men with swords. Instead, he gave them trumpets and torches, which were hidden in jars. He instructed his men to enter the camp when the Midianites were asleep and, when Gideon blew his trumpet, to break the jars containing the torches. When they did this, a loud noise was heard throughout the camp, awaking the enemy. Gideon's men yelled, "a sword for the Lord and for Gideon!" The Isrealites stood their ground and didn't attack. Terrified and confused, the Midianites began fighting each other rather than Gideon's army. Those who survived fled to the outer regions of Israel where they were captured.

THEIR VICTORY WAS DETERMINED, NOT BY THE SIZE OF THEIR ARMY, BUT BY THE SIZE OF THEIR GOD.

Gideon's story illustrates the point that God wanted his people to have faith that he would deliver on his promise to give them victory against their enemies. God wanted his people to take a stand against their enemies. Their victory was determined, not by the size of their army, but by the size of their God. The same can be said for God's people today. Our success as leaders has more to do with our decisiveness to be obedient to God's call and less to do with our individual talents.

Therefore, we should seek the Lord for instruction and have a plan of action when we find ourselves in conflict. Having a predetermined plan going into conflict keeps you from being caught off-guard and able to stand when the fighting is fierce. If you are pursuing God's will, you can have confidence that he will give you the wisdom and instruction needed for the battle. In the face of conflict, you need a battle plan. But before going to battle, you need to know who the real enemy is.

82

IDENTIFY THE REAL ENEMY

Our enemies aren't always who we think they are. An enemy will use any number of tactics to advance their cause. Rarely, does an enemy show their cards and reveal their true intentions; they often work behind the scenes, using cunning and deception. I've seen people manipulate the innocent to their advantage. Sometimes our enemies will use fear and intimidation. Other times they'll cast doubt with statements like, "How could you ever hope to change things?" or "That isn't the way the world works. You're living in a dream world. Your cause isn't worth fighting for."

While the enemies you face in leadership are numerous, there's no one more influential to your leadership than yourself. In fact, your biggest enemy as a leader may be yourself. Allow me to explain. Ideas about you and your leadership run through your mind on a daily basis. Depending on your mentality, these thoughts will either confirm God's truth or deny it. We are having conversations with ourselves all the time. If we took the time to reflect on these inner conversations, we would see how powerful they are in shaping our attitudes and actions.

Biblical counseling professor and pastor Paul Tripp speaks to this when he writes that:

> No one is more influential in your life than you are, because no one talks to you as much as you talk to yourself. People laugh at that statement, but I'm really quite serious. You're in an unending, incredibly important conversation with your soul every moment of every day. You interpret, organize, and analyze what's going on inside and outside of you. You talk to yourself about the past, you talk to yourself about the future, and you talk to yourself about what you're experiencing in the present. Obviously, this is an internal conversation—if you had this conversation aloud they would probably put you into a ward! But that's why it's so dangerous—you often don't even realize that you're saying things to yourself. But you are. You're saying things to you that will shape your desires, actions, and theology.[2]

I grew up during a time when racism was something embedded deep in the cracks of our culture. When I was six years old, I was confronted with the harsh realities of a world where the color of my skin could draw hatred from others. Cary, a white friend of mine, lived with her large family down the street from me. One afternoon, I rode my bike over to her house to ask if she could come out and play. When I knocked on her door, an older white man appeared. He was weathered, unshaven and his white hair unkempt. He stared at me behind the screen door with contempt. He swung open the door and stood in front of me without uttering a word. He had a wad of chewing tobacco in his mouth and I watched his jaw move in a long winding motion as he glared at me.

KNOW WHERE YOU WANT TO GO AND LET OTHERS KNOW WHERE YOU'RE TAKING THEM.

Frightened, I stepped back and stumbled over my feet. With each step back, he took another step forward. He looked down at me, leaned in and spit tobacco directly into my face. He never said a word to me, but his actions made it clear what he thought about me.

Humiliated, I turned around, got on my bike and drove away in tears. When I got home I slammed my bike on the ground, raced inside and hid in my bedroom. I was devastated. I didn't share that story for nearly twenty years, but it was never far from my thoughts. What happened that day would cause me to wonder for years, "Am I good enough or is what others think about me actually true?"

Years later, I recalled the story during a team-building exercise at work when we were asked to reveal any racial biases and discuss how they affected our relationships. For the first time, I gave voice to my emotions and was able to address them. What I came to see was that my experience had caused me to overextend myself in life and ministry in an attempt to prove to others that I was good enough.

For years, I didn't understand why I was drawn to dealing with issues of race and injustice and how it affected people. My childhood experience shaped me to see the issues behind people's actions. Rather than take someone's actions at face value, I wanted to probe deeper to find out what would cause someone to regard another with such disdain. The real enemy in my story was not the man himself, but the pernicious evils of racism that plagued my culture.

In his letter to the Ephesians, the Apostle Paul wrote that, "Our struggle is not against flesh and blood, but against the rulers, against the authorities, against the power of this dark world and against the spiritual forces of evil in the heavenly realms" (6:12). There is a greater enemy at work among us. This enemy not only seeks our failure, but also our destruction.

Sadly, many spend much of their time and energy fighting battles when they don't realize who the real enemy is. Therefore, do the investigative work to identify the real enemy in the battles you face. This is a critical component of your battle strategy, because we often make the mistake of confronting the attacker instead of the power behind the attack.

DETERMINE WHERE YOU WANT TO GO

Every worthwhile journey has a destination in mind. When we embark on a great journey, we hope to arrive at some kind of enjoyable place. Few, if any, would submit themselves to an arduous journey without the promise of a favorable end.

Our vision is that favorable end we hope to attain. When you have a vision fixed in our mind, it will help you traverse through the difficult terrain and setbacks during your journey. Keeping a vision at the forefront of your mind will inform your decisions and help you stay on the right path in your journey. It will also encourage you (and others) to carry on when you encounter difficulties.

Knowing where you want to go will help you discern whether a particular action will move you closer or further from your destination. When you have fixed your vision in your mind, you will develop an intuition that tells you when you're veering off path.

Pursuing your vision is an assignment that requires strategy and skill in moving people towards its fulfillment. Ultimately, it's about rallying others around God's purposes and giving them a hopeful end to work toward.

Know where you want to go and let others know where you're taking them. Give others a picture of where they're headed and what it will be like to arrive there. Great leaders know how to inspire others and give them a portrait of greater things. If you can inspire them and get them behind a vision, you will give them something that encourages them when times get tough. People need something to hope in and work towards if you expect them to spend long hours planning, strategizing and executing a vision.

Keep those that follow you up-to-date on the vision's progress. In the midst of pursuing a vision, it can be difficult to comprehend your progress. Therefore, set up markers that let others know when you've crossed an important place in the journey. Celebrate victories along the way and remind others that even greater things are ahead.

ATTACK THE ENEMY HEAD-ON

Another component of an effective battle strategy is confronting your enemy. Regardless of the size of your conflict, you must never back down in fear. Your natural reaction may be to turn away in fear. But, sooner or later, you will have to face your enemy, so it might as well be now. Take a stand and fight a good fight when it comes your way.

When Judah faced the armies of the Moabites, Ammonites and Meunites, Jehoshaphat did three important things. First, he called the people to pray and fast. Second, he led them in worship. Third, he directed them to go out against these armies singing praises to the Lord. He convinced God's people that they were prepared and empowered to face their enemies head-on.

At first glance, Jehoshaphat's plans don't make a lot of sense. How could singing praises to God be an effective strategy against such a powerful enemy? Upon further examination, however, we see great wisdom in Jehoshaphat's strategy. His actions showed that he had prepared his people for battle with the best possible defense: faith and trust in the Lord. The fight was not about Jehoshaphat or even Judah. It was about who they represented. Judah's enemies were fighting against God and the nation was crying out for God to fight for them. Like David in Psalm 35:1, their plea was: "Contend, O LORD, with those who contend with me; fight against those who fight against me!"

When the fight began over moving The Luke to a new location, I was up against a minority in the church who feared change in our growing community. Behind that fear was the bitterness, anger and resentment of past generations who had been burned and scorned by others. Perhaps they saw the move as an affront to the church's heritage, or that we were somehow erasing the church's history. To them, opposing the move was commendable, because it was preserving the church's history.

I was in a situation of obvious tension between two sides, one favoring the move and the other against it. At the same time, I was responsible to pastor this congregation, including those that opposed me. I needed to listen and understand what was happening and why it was happening. Leading the church during this time was a crucible for me personally, but it also taught me how to adjust my strategy and confront the conflict head-on.

Attacking the enemy head-on means being relentless in adversity. To be relentless is to "show no abatement of severity, intensity, strength or pace." Knowing when to press forward and be relentless is an important component of having a successful battle strategy. After I was confronted in my office and asked to leave, I knew the time had come to be relentless and press into this conflict head-on. No longer could I stand by and play from a defensive position. I needed to go on the offensive and be relentless in my pursuit of the vision God had given for this church. I didn't know every step moving forward, but I knew I couldn't back down or run away. I was going to stand!

COMMIT TO THE PLAN

You would be hard-pressed to find a better statement on commitment than the Navy SEALS' code, which states:

> I will never quit. My nation expects me to be physically harder and mentally stronger than my enemies. If knocked down, I will get back up, every time. I will draw on every remaining ounce of strength to protect my teammates and to accomplish our mission. I am never out of the fight.

Remembering this code helped me stay in the battle when it was fiercest at The Luke. The church's future was at stake and my supporters expected me (and the rest of our leadership) to stand in the midst of trial and opposition. After I was asked to resign, I formed a team with other leaders in the church to come up with a response and plan of action. We called a meeting that evening to address the situation and inform the church's members of what was happening. I was resolved not to leave and told those in attendance that I was going to stand. They responded in kind and showed their support with a standing ovation.

That meeting showed a unified front against the opposition. But the fighting only intensified from there. Not long after the meeting, I was served with a restraining order and forbidden from stepping foot on the church's property. We hired an attorney to have the restraining order lifted. When the case came to court, the judge advised our attorneys to first have a conversation. As a result, I was offered a deal by the opposition to take my people and leave the church in exchange for a severance and the newly acquired property. Taking the deal would have been the easy way out for me. But this wasn't about me. This was about God's vision for the church, and I was not about to back down and compromise over a few dollars. So we rejected the offer and the judge ruled in our favor.

ENVISION SUCCESS

When God ensured Judah that the victory was his to win, I am sure Jehoshaphat experienced a great sigh of relief. From that point forward, he could expect victory because God had guaranteed it. He could envision Judah's success against seemingly insurmountable odds. Jehoshaphat knew the history of his nation and he knew that God was reliable and trustworthy in bringing his promises to fulfillment. If God promises to do something, there isn't a force in the universe that can stop him. All that is asked of us is to stand and expect God to move.

Believing in the possibility of victory is what keeps you in the fight. Without it, you're likely to give up and accept defeat. At The Luke, I couldn't afford to see our fight as a lost cause. To be sure, there were days when it was harder to see a successful outcome in the conflict.

But I knew I had to stand regardless, because that was the only way to victory. God had assured me that I would not stand alone. He would go before me and raise up others willing to stand with me. Together, we would meet the opposition head-on.

As a leader, you have to model your confidence in God's ability to make you victorious. If they don't see it in you, how do you expect them to see it in themselves? So seek the Lord's face and expect him to give you a plan when facing conflict. Share with others your pursuit of the Lord and encourage others to do the same.

CELEBRATE IN ADVANCE

You don't have to go through conflict sulking the entire time over your situation. There is plenty of room to celebrate in life, even in times of conflict. Sometimes we need to give ourselves permission to carve out time for celebrating the Lord's goodness, regardless of our situation.

In his letter to the Philippians, Paul told them to, "rejoice in the Lord always; again I will say, rejoice" (4:4). Paul wasn't using hyperbole here. Keep in mind that he wrote his letter from prison and still makes no exceptions for *not* rejoicing in the Lord in all circumstances. How could the apostle rejoice when he was in chains? He could rejoice because he was pursuing God's vision for his life to take the gospel to the Gentiles (see Acts 22:1-21)! Paul had plenty of enemies, but that didn't keep him from celebrating the Lord's providence over his life, even if it led him to death (Phil. 1:20).

God has a vision for your leadership and wants you to celebrate him in all that you do. In Christ, we find a deeper joy that allows us to rejoice in all times because we understand that the source of our rejoicing is not our circumstances. Our source is God who is above our circumstances.

If you are working to make God's name known through your leadership, then you have every reason to celebrate. Jehoshaphat knew this and called all of Judah to celebrate with him. With his enemies approaching, Jehoshaphat bowed his face to the ground, worshiped before the Lord and called everyone in Judah to do the same (2 Chron.

20:18-19). After this, they went out to the wilderness south of Jerusalem. 2 Chronicles 20:20-23 tells us what happened next:

> And they rose early in the morning and went out into the wilderness of Tekoa. And when they went out, Jehoshaphat stood and said, "Hear me, Judah and inhabitants of Jerusalem! Believe in the LORD your God, and you will be established; believe his prophets, and you will succeed." And when he had taken counsel with the people, he appointed those who were to sing to the LORD and praise him in holy attire, as they went before the army, and say, "Give thanks to the LORD, for his steadfast love endures forever." And when they began to sing and praise, the LORD set an ambush against the men of Ammon, Moab, and Mount Seir, who had come against Judah, so that they were routed. For the men of Ammon and Moab rose against the inhabitants of Mount Seir, devoting them to destruction, and when they had made an end of the inhabitants of Seir, they all helped to destroy one another.

God responded to the praises of his people by delivering them out of the hands of their enemies. This is the climax of the story and shows us bold faith in action. Jehoshaphat's faith led him to call for a national celebration of praise and worship to God. He was certain that God was able to deliver his people and would respond to their cry for help as he had done so many times before in Israel.

Leadership is a marathon, not a sprint. It takes time to resolve conflict. You can't expect that all the complex problems you'll encounter in leadership will be fixed overnight. You must have the mindset that you're in the fight for the long haul. Along the way, there will be occasions to celebrate something wonderful and glorious that the Lord is doing. Don't pass up those opportunities, because they will re-energize you and those that follow you. It will also remind everyone that they're on the right track and give them incentive to press on and stay in the fight. Those celebrations can also serve as a foretaste of God's vision being fully realized in your organization.

If you're going to stand in the heat of the fight, you need a battle plan to advance God's vision to its completion. How you respond in the midst of conflict makes all the difference. God has called you to a task and asks you to depend on him throughout the entire process.

And he has given you an array of talents and resources to help you in the fight. Remember: fulfilling God's vision isn't a solo project. It takes a team of faithful and committed followers who are sold out on God's vision for them.

As a leader, you are called to lead others from the front. So back up what you say with what you do in leadership. Model great leadership by being the kind of leader you'd want to follow. Like Jehoshaphat, let others see you go before the Lord, worship him and pursue a God-given vision for your organization. If you're willing to put in the long hours of planning and executing, endure the hardships, rebound from setbacks and stay in the fight, then you will have given others a great example to follow.

DISCUSSION QUESTIONS

1. What steps can you take to change from a defensive position to an offensive position when faced with conflict?

2. Is being relentless part of your battle strategy? If not, how can you incorporate a relentless mindset in your strategy?

3. How do you communicate commitment to those who follow you?

4. What obstacles keep you from seeing victory? What changes to your leadership would help you (and others) see victory?

5. What did you learn from Jehoshaphat's response of celebration in the midst of conflict?

6

LEAD WITH PURPOSE

A leader is one who influences a specific group of people to move in a God-given direction.

J. ROBERT CLINTON

Leaders are intentional. They lead with purpose. Don't you think people deserve a leader who's completely devoted to his or her purpose? I do, and I want to follow someone who eats their God-given vision for breakfast, lunch and dinner. People may be smitten by a leader's charm and rhetoric for a season, but, sooner or later, that leader will be put to the test. When that happens, his or her competency (or incompetency) will be revealed.

In his bestselling book *The Purpose Driven Life* (Zondervan: 2002), Rick Warren highlights the benefits of what he calls a 'purpose driven leadership.'

- Knowing your purpose gives meaning to your life.
- Knowing your purpose simplifies your life.

- Knowing your purpose focuses your life.
- Knowing your purpose motivates your life.
- Knowing your purpose prepares you for eternity.[1]

You must have purpose in leadership and be clear about what you're doing and where you're taking others. You don't have to beg people to follow a leader with purpose—people are naturally attracted to that type of leader. We all have an innate yearning to accomplish something with our lives. Following someone who's driven to accomplish great things is alluring. That kind of drive reflects what we truly desire: for our lives to matter and be given to something worthwhile that imparts a definite purpose.

Jehoshaphat was in a desperate situation that required divine intervention. God promised deliverance, but that didn't mean his people were without responsibility in the fight. God expected Jehoshaphat to be the kind of purpose-driven leader he had called many times before in Israel's history. As king, Jehoshaphat was to model a godly posture in seeking the Lord and making decisions that reflected faith in God's power and authority.

SHOW CONFIDENCE

Joseph is a great example of purpose-driven leadership. Even in childhood, his leadership qualities were evident. Throughout his captivity in Egypt, the Lord was with Joseph and gave him favor. That favor paved the way for him to rise to one of the highest positions of authority in Egypt.

Joseph demonstrated an unshakable confidence in making decisions and never compromised his morals to get ahead in life. He was resolute in his faith and never veered off the path God put before him. He worked tirelessly to bring God honor and demonstrated leadership ability in every area of life. Regardless of the trials Joseph experienced, God gave him success because of his faith.

It's hard to get behind a leader who doesn't have confidence or believe in a vision. Joseph beamed with confidence and took each step in life knowing that it was getting him closer to fulfilling God's purposes. Joseph's faith gave him incredible strength and resolve to persevere in times of temptation and hardship.

The remarkable thing about Joseph is that he spoke confidently about his future deliverance in the midst of the trials he faced. Pharaoh saw the confidence he exuded and praised him for it. He saw the Lord's favor on him. So Pharaoh elevated Joseph to the second-highest position of authority in Egypt.

God has given you great responsibility and authority as a leader. He has entrusted you with his vision and has called you to carry it out with God-honoring excellence. Walk with humility, because God's favor—not your talents or skills—put you in this position. But also walk with confidence, because God is for you and wants to see his vision fulfilled through you.

> **GOD IS FOR YOU AND WANTS TO SEE HIS VISION FULFILLED THROUGH YOU.**

Ultimately, the goal in leadership is to bring God glory. When David went up against the giant Goliath, he was mocked and ridiculed. No one gave this young Israelite a fighting chance against such an impressive opponent. But David was confident God would give him victory that day. Rather than appeal to his ability to sling a stone, he told Goliath:

> You come to me with a sword and with a spear and with a javelin, but I come to you in the name of the LORD of hosts, the God of the armies of Israel, whom you have defied. This day the LORD will deliver you into my hand, and I will strike you down and cut off your head. And I will give the dead bodies of the host of the Philistines this day to the birds of the air and to the wild beasts of the earth, that all the earth may know that there is a God in Israel, and that all this assembly may know that the LORD saves not with sword and spear. For the battle is the LORD's, and he will give you into our hand. (1 Samuel 17:45-47)

Joseph and David were confident in their faith, because they understand that God had a specific purpose (or vision) for them. As leaders, we carry on their legacy of confidence by exercising our authority and making decisions with intentionality. If we hope to influence others towards growth and change, we need confidence to believe God is working in us to bring his purposes to pass.

ASSEMBLE YOUR TEAM

Successful leaders understand that they can't lead well on their own. They need a team behind them that's sold out to their vision and excited to work hard to see it fulfilled. Paul understood this truth well and encouraged the believers in Corinth to see that doing God's work is a team effort. In his eyes, everyone had a significant role to play; that's why he referred to believers as "co-laborers in God's service" (1 Cor. 3:9).

Any successful team needs three main things. First, a team needs a common purpose or goal to work towards. As a leader, you help define and communicate that common purpose to your teammates. Your common purpose tells people *where* you're going. Second, a team needs shared values and convictions. These shared values and convictions tell people *who* you are. They distinguish your team and give them an identity. As a leader, you have the task to reinforce this identity as often as you can. Third, a team needs freedom and flexibility to work and change without compromising its stated purpose. This tells people *how* you'll achieve your purpose. Ideally, you want your team to be a dynamic collection of talented and dedicated men and women. Within this diverse group, there needs to be room for the exchange of ideas on how to achieve your goal. People want to be on a team where they are heard and understood. Essentially, they want to know (in tangible ways) that their work is contributing to the team's success. As a leader, you are responsible to encourage others to work together within this dynamic framework to achieve God's purpose.

Every team needs leadership. Every team needs someone to understand the group's dynamics and synthesize various ideas from teammates into solutions. In the end, decisions need to be made and plans need to be put into action. Teammates will disagree on the best way to achieve a goal and that's okay. Diversity on a team helps see problems and solutions from multiple angles. Your job as a leader is to facilitate these discussions and decide which solution is the best—and most appropriate—way to get the team closer to its goal.

Aside from a task force put together to achieve a short-term goal, it's likely that your team will change over time. In every organization, people come and go as much as seasons change. Sometimes people move in different directions and leave the team. Accept the changing nature of leadership and get the most out of the people on your team in any given circumstance. When you do this, you won't try to recreate every great team you've been on before and will work within the means that God has given you for that time.

Every leader needs to decide who best fits on his or her team. To make this decision, leaders need to be in sync with their vision and instinctively know who would help the team make that vision come to pass. In his book, *Instinct: The Power to Unleash Your Inborn Drive* (FaithWords: 2014), Bishop T. D. Jakes describes what he calls 'instinctive leadership:'

> While no two leaders are exactly the same and each will vary their style and method, all individuals leading by instinct explore the distance between where they've been and where they're going. Some approach leadership based on their strength or the strength of the team, others on their previous organization's culture or the culture that was established when they got there. They inherit systems and struggles that in no way resemble the vision and mandate that they are most passionate about. They must then decide: who stays and who goes.[2]

Always consult your team about decisions and give them a platform to give you feedback. Proverbs 15:22 says that, "Plans fail for lack of counsel, but with many advisers they succeed." You have a host of talents surrounding you. Use them! You never know the wealth you have right in your midst if you're unwilling to look for it. Be mindful not to throw away or ignore the resources God has given you to fulfill his vision.

Spend time getting to know your team. Get to know them personally and listen to their stories by creating opportunities for fellowship. It might be over dinner, bowling or running errands. Whatever the occasion, give them the freedom and comfort to share their lives with you. When you listen with sincerity, you let them know they are valuable to you as a person and teammate.

BE A GOOD BOSS

What kind of boss do you want to work for? Whatever comes to mind, that's the kind of boss you need to be for others. There are few things more frustrating than working for someone who doesn't value your opinion, is inflexible, short-tempered and hard to work with. If someone enjoys working for their boss, the chances of them burning out or quitting significantly drops.

In *Climbing the Executive Ladder* (McGraw-Hill: 1950), George Kienzle and Edward Dare write that, "Few things will pay you bigger dividends than the time and trouble you take to understand people. Nothing will give you greater satisfaction or bring you more happiness."[3] Author Laurie Beth Jones defines a good boss as one who recognizes that he or she has "a God-given responsibility to nurture and develop their employees. Good bosses are sensitive to the needs of their workers and are always looking for ways to promote their station in life."[4] Jones cites Jesus and Nehemiah as prime examples of those that served their authorities faithfully, because they had integrity and a desire to honor God. Another quality these biblical bosses fostered in their leadership was trust.[5]

> THE GOAL IN LEADERSHIP IS NOT BE THE MOST POPULAR LEADER. IT'S TO DO WHAT'S RIGHT. IT'S TO BE A MAN OR WOMAN OF INTEGRITY.

Being a good boss wasn't easy at The Luke because deep-seated bitterness and resentment in the church had created the wrong perception of leadership. As a result, a fight for control in the church ensued that threatened its future. Essentially, the power struggle boiled down to this—those opposed to us moving the church were afraid the church's heritage would be lost. So they did everything they could to undermine the move.

Unfortunately, they were under the impression that a good boss was anyone that would do as they are told, simply managing the church to keep things moving along as they always had. Anything short of that was unacceptable. I knew I couldn't be that kind of boss for them nor was I called to be that kind of boss. Remember: not everyone has to consider you a good boss. You're not responsible for others' opinions of you as a boss. What you are responsible for is being a good boss in God's eyes.

LEADERSHIP AND SACRIFICE

Be prepared for God to ask you to sacrifice in your leadership. Seeking to obey God and fulfill his vision means that you will have to die to yourself daily. My story taught me this truth a hundred times over. Sacrifice in leadership means setting aside small, selfish ambitions for greater ones. It means forgoing the praise and approval of others in preference to God's praise and approval. You will make many hard choices on the path of leadership. Sometimes it will cost you money, prestige and relationships. Provided you are seeking the Lord as a leader, you can rest assured that those sacrifices will pay off in the end. The goal in leadership is not be the most popular leader. It's to do what's right. It's to be a man or woman of integrity. It's to lead others where God wants them to go, regardless of the opinions of others.

In the face of conflict at The Luke, I was learning the cost of discipleship and how much God demanded of his leaders. Many were watching things unfold at our church and I wanted them to see that our fight was worth sacrificing for. Why? Because it was God's vision for the church and accomplishing it would cost us all something. There's no way around the truth that following Christ means setting aside your agenda for his. That was the message Jesus gave to the Rich Young Ruler in Matthew 19:16-30. That's the message he gives his followers today.

My experience at The Luke was my training ground for developing Christ-like character in my leadership. I learned the value of discipleship and what it looked like to be deliberate in training and preparing others to do God's work as Jesus did. Granted, I'm not perfect, but in the midst of my failures and flaws I learned that I needed to feast on God's Word and petition him in prayer all the more. If you want to be a godly leader, you must follow the Jesus path. It's not the easiest path and it will cost you everything. However, there's nothing more rewarding and satisfying than tracing the Savior's footsteps.

God honors our sacrifices. When we're willing to step out and give everything to him, he responds by giving us what we need to do his work. The community of believers is a great resource for God's leaders. There, you can find encouragement and motivation to keep moving forward. The support I received from The Luke's members gave me the strength I needed to stand in dark and difficult times. Together, we celebrated, grieved and co-labored in pursuit of a God-given vision. I was called to shepherd them through this conflict, but they also cared for me in countless ways that fill me with thanks and gratitude to this day.

ENCOURAGEMENT AND REST

We all grow weary and need encouragement to press on. For leaders, it's important to encourage those who follow you, especially in the midst of battle. Build them up and speak truth into their lives. Show them you value their hard work. Yes, leaders want to accomplish things, but that doesn't mean working yourself (and others) to death. Hard work is commendable, but there's no glory in being a workaholic.

Set aside time to have a Sabbath day and recharge spiritually, emotionally and physically. God rested on the seventh day after he had created the world and called his people to do the same. Jesus took time away from his work to rest. If he needed it, what makes us think we don't? When we refuse to rest, we're essentially communicating that we don't trust God with the results; that we need to work harder, because it all depends on us. That's faith in yourself and your abilities, not in God.

When you have your Sabbath, understand the main purposes of that time: to worship God and enjoy some necessary rest and recreation. Encourage others in your organization to do the same. Play with your kids. Go out to eat with friends. Take your wife on a date. Enjoy the pleasures this life has to offer and thank God for his goodness and faithfulness to you.

Celebrating progress is another way for you and those in your organization to recharge. Be intentional about creating positive and memorable experiences for others to remember little and big victories along the way. In the Old Testament, the Israelites created altars to serve as memorials of God's loving presence and saving activity in the lives of his people. Those altars were symbols of God's faithfulness.

Building altars today can be a powerful way to remember God's care over your leadership and organization. At The Luke, we had a dedication ceremony when we broke ground on the church's new property. Hundreds showed up that day and joy filled the air as we talked about the future of the church. We prayed over the land and consecrated it as a place of worship and blessing. We thanked God for his past faithfulness and looked forward with confidence to him doing great things at that spot. Like Jehoshaphat, we took time in the midst of conflict to take a stand by worshiping and singing praises to God. Many members have told me afterward that the ceremony encouraged them to keep fighting and persevere in adversity.

TESTED LEADERSHIP

When you lead with purpose, you will be tested. This is without exception because we live in a world that doesn't want God's plans to succeed. Therefore, prepare yourself to be tested. Understand that you may be attacked, maligned or even ignored as a leader. Also understand that God has given you everything you need to stand when tested: "His divine power has given us everything we need for a godly life through our knowledge of him who called us by his own glory and goodness" (2 Pet. 1:3).

Along with this, God has promised never to put you in a situation where you can't persevere: "No temptation has overtaken you that is not common to man. God is faithful, and he will not let you be tempted beyond your ability, but with the temptation he will also provide the way of escape, that you may be able to endure it" (1 Cor. 10:13).

A few weeks before the new church building was completed, one of our deacons was hospitalized. The diagnosis was not good. The doctors feared that his death was imminent. As a pastor, I visit the sick in our church on a weekly basis. However, the thought of visiting this deacon was a test because he was in the group that confronted me and tried to fire me. His actions had brought me frustration, pain and many sleepless nights. Now he was possibly on his deathbed and I wasn't sure what to do. Another deacon was insistent that I visit him. He was right. We had both been through a lot and I knew we needed to talk if we hoped to heal our relationship and put the past where it belonged.

It was a long walk to the deacon's hospital room. Thoughts of the past turned over in my mind. I was angry and hurt. I felt betrayed by this man. Then, I heard a still, small voice within me say, "This isn't about you." The tension inside me disappeared and I felt a peace come over me. I entered the hospital room and saw the deacon lying on his bead. A smile broke across his face when he saw me. After a short exchange of small talk, the other deacons in the room left to give the two of us time alone.

KNOW THAT GOD HAS A PURPOSE BEHIND EVERY ADVERSE SITUATION YOU FACE AS A LEADER.

We talked honestly and openly about the past. It wasn't easy, but it was right for us to have the conversation. Then, I said, "What's in the past is in the past. You've done a lot for this church. I know your family has been instrumental in the life of this church from its founding." Tears started to roll down his cheeks as I spoke further, "I know this church means a lot to you. I promise that I'm not going to let the history of this church fade away." After I was finished, he took my hand and clenched it. We sat in silence for a moment. Then I asked him to share the church's history with me.

For the next hour, he recounted the history of The Luke. He shared defining moments and key figures that left a legacy of faith in the church. The time seemed to pass by in a blink. As I got up to leave, I told him I loved him. "I love you too, pastor," he replied. He looked me in the eye and said, "Do well. Make me proud." Our hearts were no longer heavy in that moment. Grace had broken through the pain and hurt to bring healing. The conflict between us was over and we could move forward.

In the Bible, God's leaders were tested often. Moses was challenged by rebel factions and even his own siblings. Absalom, David's son, tried to usurp his father's throne. Jesus was tested in the wilderness before he inaugurated his ministry. How did these leaders pass the test? By staying in tune with the voice of God. That was the deciding factor that gave them perseverance when put to the test.

When you're tested, see it as an opportunity to strengthen your character and leadership. Know that God has a purpose behind every adverse situation you face as a leader. In writing to the believers in Rome, Paul points to this purpose with these encouraging words: "We rejoice in our sufferings, knowing that suffering produces endurance, and endurance produces character, and character produces hope, and hope does not put us to shame" (Rom. 5:3-5). Peter also spoke to the refining quality of our testing when he wrote:

> In [your salvation] rejoice, though now for a little while, if necessary, you have been grieved by various trials, so that the tested genuineness of your faith—more precious than gold that perishes though it is tested by fire—may be found to result in praise and glory and honor at the revelation of Jesus Christ. (1 Pet. 1:6-7)

Don't be discouraged when your leadership is tested. Remember: it comes with the job of being a leader. Stay the course, and stick with God's plan. He has given you everything you need to persevere in the fight. He's entrusted you with his vision and doesn't want you to fight alone. Assemble a team of dedicated individuals that will use their personalities and talents to achieve the vision. Take advantage of the support on your team and in your organization; know that you have individuals who want to see you succeed and see God's vision come to fruition.

A great battle plan is indispensable in leadership. It sets down tracks for moving your organization successfully through conflict. Leading with purpose stokes the fire that lights the way. However, when the fighting starts, your giants will come calling and your fears will begin to surface. Fear has put many so-called leaders on the sideline. If you're going to lead well and execute your plan, you must face your fears.

DISCUSSION QUESTIONS

1. What is stopping you from having the confidence you need to be an effective leader? What would help you get over these obstacles?

2. What qualities do you look for in assembling an effective team?

3. How have others encouraged you in your leadership? How have you encouraged others recently in your leadership?

4. What does it take for a leader to stay committed to a vision? Be specific.

7

FACE YOUR FEARS

You gain strength, courage, and confidence by every experience in which you really stop to look fear in the face. You must do the thing, which you think you cannot do.

ELEANOR ROOSEVELT

reviously, we established that we face a great enemy in our leadership. This enemy doesn't want us to succeed in doing God's purposes and will use any means necessary to stop us. The enemy's arsenal is plentiful. In his work, *Precious Remedies Against Satan's Devices* (Banner of Truth Press: 1968), seventeenth century Puritan Thomas Brooks wrote about our enemy's many strategies:

> Several devices [the enemy] has to draw souls to sin, and several plots he has to keep souls from all holy and heavenly services, and [strategies] he has to keep souls in mourning, staggering, doubting and questioning condition. He has several devices to destroy the great and honorable, the wise and learned, the blind and ignorant, the rich and the poor,

the real and the nominal Christians.

The enemy knows you. He knows where you're weak and will attack you in those vulnerable places. One of the most dangerous weapons the enemy uses against God's people is fear. The term *fear* deserves some clarification. There are two kinds of fear: 1) the kind that fills us with dread and paralyzes us, and 2) the kind that fills us with reverence for God, for who he is and what he does. The enemy wants to fill us with the first kind of fear. God wants to fill us with the second kind, because it draws us closer to him in times of trouble, confusion and uncertainty.

> ONE OF THE MOST DANGEROUS WEAPONS THE ENEMY USES AGAINST GOD'S PEOPLE IS FEAR.

Fear from the enemy can clobber us like a mallet if we let it. His fear will deliver heavy blows that cause us anxiety and indecision in our lives. When we allow this type of fear to hold sway over us, it will keep us up at night; it will fill us with terror about the future; it will cast all kinds of doubts on our abilities to achieve what we've been called to do. It short, this kind of fear will pummel us into submission and send us running from the fight.

The enemy's goal is to paralyze us—to keep us from taking a stand. His fear plays in our mind like a record on the turntable. Round and round it goes, reinforcing lies and causing you to doubt yourself and God. The only way to overcome the enemy's strategy is to combat it with the right kind of fear.

Really, the question is not, "Will I fear?" but "Whom will I fear?" In his book, *All That Jesus Asks* (Baker Books: 2010), Stan Guthrie addresses this key question:

> Fear *will* come, no matter what. Fear is a fact of any thinking person's existence. But it matters supremely what the object of our fear is. Jesus says that since we are going to fear anyway, it makes more sense to fear God, not men [or our circumstances].[1]

Fear of God takes the needle off that record of discouragement and accusation that the enemy wants to keep playing. When you refuse to listen to fear, you will start listening to hope. Hope in God casts out the enemy's fear. It looks to the future with expectation of greater things to come for God's people. It opens up your imagination to see wonderful possibilities in your life. It fills you with confidence to stand when things don't go according to plan or in the face of opposition. Ultimately, fear in God will direct your heart to your greatest refuge—Jesus. Sweeter words I do not know than the lyric from Charles Wesley's hymn 'O For a Thousand Tongues to Sing' that tells us that Jesus is "the name that charms our fears."

Jehoshaphat had to face his fears when confronted by his enemies. Fear filled the king's heart when he heard that the armies of the Moabites, Ammonites and Meunites were marching towards Judah. But Jehoshaphat refused to let fear grip his heart. In response to his fear, he ran to the one true Source of strength and found refuge there. He knew only God could rescue Judah from the hands of her enemies. He had the right kind of fear in the situation; rather than be paralyzed by fear, his fear caused him to act. Scripture tells us that he "set his face to seek the LORD, and proclaimed a fast throughout all Judah. And Judah assembled to seek help from the LORD; from all the cities of Judah they came to seek the LORD" (2 Chron. 20:3-4).

Fear is a natural response when there's danger and uncertainty. In leadership, you will encounter circumstances that cause you to fear. Knowing how to respond to fear will set you apart as a true leader. Goliath was a giant that tried to strike fear into the heart of David. But David took a stand against the mighty giant. He faced Goliath with another kind of fear—fear in God. That fear gave him victory on the battlefield that day. The same can be true for you. You must take a stand against the enemy's fear tactics and appeal to the victory you have in Jesus (1 Cor. 15:57).

DON'T AVOID YOUR FEARS

Another strategy of the enemy is to keep our fears hidden from view. Early in life, our culture tells us that fear equals weakness. So we overcompensate with a fearless front to mask our insecurities and weaknesses. We think the courageous are those without fear. But courage is not the absence of fear; it's the ability to stand in the face of fear. When you keep your fears hidden, you miss the point that facing your fears is an essential component of your growth as a leader. Moreover, it's necessary in fulfilling God's purposes for you.

I wondered whether I could handle the conflict we were experiencing at The Luke. Insecurities and feelings of inadequacy that originated in childhood began to surface as the fight intensified. I was under attack, and the enemy was aiming at the place where I was most vulnerable. I began hearing the familiar tune whose lyrics told me, "You're not good enough and never will be," and "It's only a matter of time before everyone finds out who you *really* are. You better hide how you really feel or you'll be exposed."

Identifying an attack takes knowledge of the enemy and yourself. If you understand how the enemy operates and where you're vulnerable, you can expect to be attacked at those weak points. The enemy might attack you with accusations. When those accusations come, they come loaded with shame. The source of that shame is often from past sins and mistakes. On the other hand, he might try to fill you with pride and encourage you to act on your own strength rather than seek the Lord. Hopefully, these few examples show you just how deceptive and serious the enemy is in his work.

When you face your fears, take time to ask some honest questions:
- What am I really afraid of here?
- Why am I afraid?
- How am I vulnerable to attack?
- What lies or accusations is the enemy trying to plant in my mind?

Answering these questions is not enough, however. You need to respond with God's truth and promises:

> God is bigger than this situation and bigger than my fears.
> Jesus calls me to fear God rather than men. Because I am a
> child of God, I have no reason to fear the enemy. The enemy
> is a liar and accuser that only seeks my destruction. Only in
> Christ can I find strength to face my fears, overcome them and
> find victory in this fight.

If I was going to lead our church through the conflict we were facing, I was going to have to be honest about the fears I was experiencing. Refusing to be honest would mean that I preferred running from these fears. It would also show that I didn't trust the vision God had given me for the church.

The enemy can shackle a person with a defeated attitude and reluctance to take a stand for fear of rejection or failure. Don't succumb to the enemy's strategies. Respond to his cunning by seeking the Lord for a strength that will withstand the onslaught of attack. You can't fight the enemy in your own strength, and God never intended for you to fight alone. Jehoshaphat knew this and responded accordingly. God is with you in conflict and gives you the tools and wisdom needed to face your fears. In Christ, we are capable of so much more than we realize. The words of children's author A.A. Milne speak to this incredible truth: "Promise me you'll always remember: You're braver than you believe, and stronger than you seem, and smarter than you think."

ADMIT YOUR FEARS AND REJECT REJECTION

When we're honest about our fears and insecurities, we liberate ourselves to trust God with the results of our situations. In need, we look to him for provision. It's okay to admit that you're afraid, because fear is natural. Denying that you're afraid will only give the enemy an advantage against you. Channel your fear in the right direction—towards God and his ability to give you victory.

The wrong kind of fear gripped me for years. In the heat of conflict, those fears were magnified to where they could no longer be ignored. My lack of confidence was affecting my confidence in the Lord. If I was going to stand, I needed to address my fears head-on. I had to take an honest look at my past and discover the root of my fears.

As a child, I struggled with rejection. Always asking the question, "Am I good enough?" It wasn't until I revisited my past that I saw how the enemy used my experience against me. When the deacon board gave me my dismissal letter, I was taken right back to childhood and those feelings of rejection. Despite my best efforts to work hard and lead the church well, they were rejecting me. Or so I thought. The truth was that I was projecting my feelings of rejection from the past onto the deacon board. As I struggled with these doubts and fears, I knew I had to move past them in order to fulfill God's calling.

If you want to walk in the fullness of God's purposes for your life, you must break free from the fear that paralyzes you and the doubts that question your identity. Expose the enemy's lies and bring them out into the light. Like Jehoshaphat, seek the Lord's face when fear grips you. Acknowledge your fear, and seek the assistance necessary to overcome your fears.

BE TRANSPARENT

David showed great bravery against Goliath. His story shows us he was a valiant warrior for God, from the time he was a shepherd boy to his reign as Israel's king. But there was another side to David. He was also a poet. He wrote half the psalms in the Bible, and each of them confirms God's view of David as "a man after his own heart" (1 Sam. 13:14). David expresses the full range of emotions throughout his psalms: they are filled with love, tenderness, intimacy, grief, regret, lament, anger, fear and doubt. This warrior-poet was transparent in his conversations with God and looked to him for strength, comfort, direction and deliverance from his enemies.

We would do well to follow David's lead and approach God as transparently as he did. God already knows you inside and out. In fact, he knows you better than you know yourself. So, you can leave shame at the door when you enter his house and talk to him. Every good thing about you (i.e., your personality, gifts, talents) can be attributed to the Lord's handiwork. And he has measured out every single day of your life to serve his purposes. David attests to God's intimate knowledge of us when he writes in Psalm 139:13-16:

> For you formed my inward parts;
> you knitted me together in my mother's womb.
> I praise you, for I am fearfully and wonderfully made.
> Wonderful are your works;
> my soul knows it very well.

> My frame was not hidden from you,
> when I was being made in secret,
> intricately woven in the depths of the earth.
> Your eyes saw my unformed substance;
> in your book were written, every one of them,
> the days that were formed for me,
> when as yet there was none of them.

Not only can you be transparent with God, you can also be transparent with others about your struggles, fears, doubts and insecurities. Let others see you wrestle with these in an honest and open way. Seek the appropriate time and place for sharing, and invite others to pray over the situation. God doesn't call his leaders to be superheroes. He knows they doubt, struggle, fail and grow weary. Being transparent with others will show them that the only way to overcome fear is to address it and bring it before the Lord.

Rather than hinder, transparency has the power to transform your leadership in remarkable ways. Take the golden opportunity to show others the real *you* in the midst of trials and conflict. In the words of Suzy Wetlaufer: "Sometimes you have to be worn out and burnt out to become authentic and original."[2]

Those who follow will not benefit if all you do is *talk* about fighting. They need to see you fighting alongside them and for them. Jesus sweated blood in the Garden of Gethsemane on the night of his betrayal. Jesus knew that fulfilling God's vision would eventually lead him to the Cross, and he was resolved to press on when the fight was intense and the struggle real. Are you prepared to daily take up your cross and follow him (Luke 9:23)? Do others see you contending for your God-given vision and for them? If so, you're setting a wonderful example for them to follow.

If those you lead see you weep over broken relationships in a conflict, you'll give them permission to weep over broken relationships in their lives. If they see you going before the Lord in a desperate situation, you'll show them what real trust looks like.

Under the harsh light of conflict, the emotional toll it was taking on me was becoming evident to everyone involved. The church needed to know that my heart was heavy and that I was battle-worn. I could've been prideful and tried to stuff my fears and struggles, but that would have only given the enemy an advantage. If you're going to face the enemy (and your fears), you need to do it in the light. Fighting in the dark is home territory for the enemy. Don't give him the home-field advantage. Bring your struggles out into the light and let others minister to you. Remember: God doesn't want you to struggle alone.

The beautiful thing about my situation is that God allowed me to be weak before those I was leading. In response, they were strong for me in that moment. Their support gave me newfound strength and motivation to stay in the fight. Don't believe the lie that being weak before others is bad leadership. On the contrary, being weak shows that you're human. People are drawn to authentic leaders that are approachable. People can relate to you when you're transparent, because they see that you struggle too.

DEALING WITH DEPRESSION

You may be surprised to know that many leaders experience seasonal or prolonged depression in the course of their leadership. In working with many leaders in various fields over the years, I've found this to be true.

Depression is a disorder that can have multiple causes. Psychological, biological and environmental factors (or some combination of the three) may contribute to its development. Depression ranges from mild to more severe forms. Depression affects the way you think, feel and behave. It can also lead to multiple emotional and physical problems.

Depression is more than a bout with melancholy or simply going through an emotional funk. It's a persistent sadness or loss of interest that doesn't seem to lift on its own. Symptoms for depression include: sad or empty feelings, decreased interest or pleasure in activities, noticeable changes in sleep, appetite and energy, feelings of worthlessness or guilt, being agitated easily or slowed down in daily activity, difficulty thinking or concentrating, thoughts of death or suicide.

Sometimes depression is onset by a difficult circumstance or major change (e.g., conflict, death, etc.). Sometimes its specific cause is unknown, even when one seeks counseling and/or medical treatment. There are other times when depression is caused by what the fifteenth-century writer Saint John of the Cross called the "dark night of the soul."

This dark night of the soul is a time of spiritual drought when God removes all sense of comfort from a believer for the purpose of drawing him or her into greater devotion to and intimacy with him. Experienced by pastors and laypeople alike, it is a period when God lovingly strips away our superficial comforts and multiple distractions to reveal himself as our true Comforter and Source of Joy. It is a painful—but necessary—process that strengthens our character and commitment to God's purposes. While God has not abandoned the believer, he or she may feel that he has. Depression often accompanies these feelings of abandonment. Such was the feeling experienced by the psalmist in Psalm 88 when he declared, "You have put me in the depths of the pit, in the regions dark and deep" (v.6). He goes on to exclaim in vv.13-18:

> But I, O LORD, cry to you;
> in the morning my prayer comes before you.
> O LORD, why do you cast my soul away?
> Why do you hide your face from me?
> Afflicted and close to death from my youth up,
> I suffer your terrors; I am helpless.
> Your wrath has swept over me;
> your dreadful assaults destroy me.
> They surround me like a flood all day long;
> they close in on me together.
> You have caused my beloved and my friend to shun me;
> my companions have become darkness.

There aren't many contemporary praise songs based on Psalm 88, because it reveals another side of the Christian walk that many of us overlook. What the psalmist speaks to is a very real experience that countless believers have gone through. When we experience the dark night of the soul and the depression that often accompanies it, we have a choice—to avoid it or accept it. Richard Foster implores us to accept it as God's good work:

> When God lovingly draws us into a dark night of the soul,
> there is often a temptation to seek release from it and to
> blame everyone and everything for our inner dullness. The
> preacher is such a bore. The hymn singing is too weak. The

worship service is so dull. We may begin to look around for another church or a new experience to give us 'spiritual goose bumps.' This is a serious mistake. Recognize the dark night for what it is. Be grateful that God is lovingly drawing you away from every distraction so that you can see him clearly. Rather than chafing and fight [against it], become still and wait.[3]

If you are a leader who's pursuing God's vision for your life, chances are you will experience your own dark night of the soul (if you haven't already). The dark night often precedes a major change or venture you are about to embark on as a leader. During my season of conflict at The Luke, I experienced my own dark night of the soul.

Being a pastor is not easy. Like most jobs, it comes with its fair share of stress and frustration. Week in and week out I am called to handle the demands of my congregation, which include preaching, teaching and counseling others. Daily, I have to confront the brokenness of this world in our church and community. Along with this, I'm also dealing with my own brokenness.

The ongoing conflict surrounding our decision to move the church across town was having an affect on me. Dealing with this conflict and juggling my pastoral responsibilities at the same time started to weigh on me. Brick by brick, the load got heavier and, before long, I began to sink into a deep depression. Getting out of bed became a struggle. I could function and perform my duties as a pastor, but the motivation and drive wasn't there. The things that used to bring me comfort and joy had little to no effect.

Upon reflection, I see that God was drawing me into the dark night. For a while, I suffered in silence. I was afraid to reveal my struggle. I thought I could endure it alone and that it would pass. But it didn't. It wasn't long before the depression started to affect others in my life, particularly my family. Physically, I was present, but my thoughts and emotions were elsewhere.

When I saw that my depression wouldn't go away on its own, I sought help. First, I confided in my wife and then a therapist. Giving voice to my depression and sharing my experience with others was the first step in addressing the issue. After this, I opened up to other pastors and leaders about my depression. Many of them could relate to what I was going through. I found comfort in knowing depression wasn't uncommon and that many in leadership positions have had to deal with it. Slowly, I began to see the spiritual benefits of my experience; that God was giving me this season of depression to draw me closer to him and to help me relate to the countless others dealing with it.

Dealing with depression can be complex, because it manifests differently in people. However, there are some helpful things you can do when you experience depression. First, don't isolate yourself. Keeping depression hidden from view will only allow it to fester and cause more damage. In the midst of depression, the enemy will try and isolate you from others. Therefore, counterattack and be open about your depression. Invite trusted others to join you in the struggle and seek help in the right places.

> I FOUND COMFORT IN KNOWING DEPRESSION WASN'T UNCOMMON AND THAT MANY IN LEADERSHIP POSITIONS HAVE HAD TO DEAL WITH IT.

Second, keep the lines of communication open with God. Spend time in God's Word and prayer, even when you don't feel like it. Make it a daily discipline and look at the time as getting your daily nourishment. Without it, you'll grow weak and your condition will get worse, not better. The desire may not be there. So pray for the desire.

How did Jesus respond to Satan when he was tempted in his own dark night of the soul in the wilderness? He responded by appealing to God's Word! He was fasting and forgoing the comforts of food when the enemy tempted him to turn stones into bread. To this, Jesus told the enemy: "Man shall not live by bread alone, but by every word that comes from the mouth of God" (Matt. 4:4). Therefore, feast upon God's Word and seek his light in the darkness.

Third, take time to examine yourself. Depression has a way of revealing things about us we wouldn't normally see. If we pay attention, depression can reveal our weaknesses, blind spots, idols, ulterior motives, prejudices, biases, defense mechanisms, etc. As a leader, it's important not only to see these issues, but also address them.

In addition, it's important to see your depression in light of how God sees you. Consider the many blessings you have as an adopted child in God's family! You have a new relationship with God that is marked by unfailing love and acceptance. His love for you is never extinguished, not even by something like depression. You are precious in his sight, and he walks with you through the depression. When your enemies and depressive thoughts condemn you, you must cling to the promise that God's love has freed you from condemnation and into new life:

> If God is for us, who can be against us? He who did not spare his own Son but gave him up for us all, how will he not also with him graciously give us all things? Who shall bring any charge against God's elect? It is God who justifies. Who is to condemn? Christ Jesus is the one who died—more than that, who was raised—who is at the right hand of God, who indeed is interceding for us. Who shall separate us from the love of Christ? Shall tribulation, or distress, or persecution, or famine, or nakedness, or danger, or sword? As it is written, "For your sake we are being killed all the day long; we are regarded as sheep to be slaughtered." No, in all these things we are more than conquerors through him who loved us. For I am sure that neither death nor life, nor angels nor rulers, nor things present nor things to come, nor powers, nor height nor depth, nor anything else in all creation, will be able to separate us from the love of God in Christ Jesus our Lord. (Romans 8:31-39)

God is not unaware of your condition. If you're experiencing depression, it isn't without purpose. You may not know what that purpose is right now. But, in time, God will reveal himself and cause the darkness to lift. In the meantime, don't waste your experience. In the raging current of depression, reach out and take hold of the lifebuoy of God's promises and the community of faith he's given you. Share in your afflictions with them and share in your comforts also. As 2 Corinthians 1:3-5 tells us:

> Blessed be the God and Father of our Lord Jesus Christ, the Father of mercies and God of all comfort, who comforts us in all our affliction, so that we may be able to comfort those who are in any affliction, with the comfort with which we

ourselves are comforted by God. For as we share abundantly in Christ's sufferings, so through Christ we share abundantly in comfort too.

SPEAK TRUTH OVER YOUR LIFE

The Word of God is powerful. That's what the author of Hebrews tells us when he writes: "The word of God is living and active, sharper than any two-edged sword, piercing to the division of soul and of spirit, of joints and of marrow, and discerning the thoughts and intentions of the heart" (4:12). Words have incredible power. God created the universe by speaking it into existence. As his creation, we also have the power to speak life (or death) with our words. Proverbs 18:21 says, "The tongue has the power of life and death, and those who love it will eat its fruit." Your words will be poison or fruit, depending on how you use them. James 3:1-12 is another passage that shows the destructive power of the unbridled tongue.

Before facing his enemies, Jehoshaphat went before the Lord in prayer. In Jerusalem's temple and before all Judah, Jehoshaphat petitioned the Lord and appealed to his Word, which revealed his saving character and recalled stories of past deliverance:

O LORD, God of our fathers, are you not God in heaven? You rule over all the kingdoms of the nations. In your hand are power and might, so that none is able to withstand you. Did you not, our God, drive out the inhabitants of this land before your people Israel, and give it forever to the descendants of Abraham your friend? And they have lived in it and have built for you in it a sanctuary for your name, saying, "If disaster comes upon us, the sword, judgment, or pestilence, or famine, we will stand before this house and before you— for your name is in this house—and cry out to you in our affliction, and you will hear and save."

And now behold, the men of Ammon and Moab and Mount Seir, whom you would not let Israel invade when they came from the land of Egypt, and whom they avoided and did not destroy—behold, they reward us by coming to drive us out of your possession, which you have given us to inherit. O our God, will you not execute judgment on them? For we are powerless against this great horde that is coming against us. We do not know what to do, but our eyes are on you. (2 Chronicles 20:6-12)

Jehoshaphat knew God's Word, and he knew the stories of God's redemption that had been passed down for generations in Israel. That's why he could go before the Lord and make such a bold request; he knew God had given his people victory in the past and was capable of doing it in the future. The Bible is full of God's promises. When you find yourself in an intense battle (be it internal or external), remind yourself of who God is and what he has promised. Find encouragement in the stories of past saints and how they overcame fear and adversity and saw victory, because they turned to God in their darkest hour. If the weight of your circumstance causes you to sink, make a list of what you're afraid of and respond to each item with a promise from Scripture.

FIGHT TO SPEAK TRUTH INTO YOUR LIFE AND TO THOSE WHO FOLLOW YOU.

His promises will lift you up and give you certainty that the outcome in your situation will bring him glory and grow you as a leader.

Before he became king, David was a fugitive on the run from King Saul. He was God's choice to be Israel's next king, but God led his servant through a difficult time of testing and hardship on his path to the throne. In 1 Samuel 30, David and his men came to Ziklag and camped there. While David and his men were away from Ziklag, the Amalekites raided Ziklag, burned it the ground and took the wives, sons, daughters, livestock and valuables belonging to David and his men. When they returned to their camp, they were so distraught that they fell on their knees and wept until they had no more strength to weep. The men were so embittered that they wanted to stone David. But David strengthened himself in the Lord and prayed about whether to pursue the Amalekites. God promised David that he would recover everything if he pursued his enemies. David, along with six hundred men, set out in hot pursuit of the Amalekites. When he came to the place where they were encamped, he fought them from twilight to evening the next day. He overcame his enemy and retrieved the families and possessions that had been taken captive.

David stayed in constant communion with the Lord as a leader. When he was in a life-threatening situation, he didn't run from danger. He ran to God and asked him what he should do. He knew God could give him victory, and he asked God to bless him in overtaking the Amalekites and taking back what was rightfully Israel's.

Consistently meditating on God's Word plants his truth and promises firmly in your mind. Sometimes you need to go on the offensive against the enemy. Act. Speak. Declare God's truth about him and you. You might say something like, "Self, God says you're more than a conqueror (Rom. 8:37)! Self, God says you're the head and not the tail (Deut. 28:13)! Self, God says greater is he that is in you than he that is in the world (1 John 4:4)! Self, God says you shall live and not die (Psalm 118:17)!"

Speak against the enemy's lies by appealing to God's promises to you, namely that you are his child and have his affection and favor. Speak truth over the situation; hold fast to the truth that in Christ you have all you need to live a full and godly life. Fear and depression cannot overcome you if you choose to combat them with God's Word. Follow Jesus' model and use God's Word as your sword. Fight to speak truth into your life and to those who follow you.

Regardless of your inner conflict, find the courage to stand in the battle by admitting your fears and being transparent about them, praying earnestly for God to move in and through you, addressing any besetting depression and encouraging yourself (and others) with God's Word.

Primarily, this book is about how to take a stand and lead through conflict. But what do you do *after* the conflict is over? How do you lead others after the dust on the battlefield has settled? What does it look like to come off the field of combat and enter a new phase in your leadership? The next chapter will answer those questions and provide you with helpful suggestions for maximizing your leadership in a new season of recovery and restoration after conflict.

DISCUSSION QUESTIONS

1. What are some practical ways for you to address your fears? With whom will you share these fears?

2. Do you find it hard to be transparent with others about your struggles? Why or why not?

3. Have you personally experienced depression before? When did it become an issue and how did you address it?

4. Have you experienced what St. John of the Cross called the "dark night of the soul?" If so, how did God grow you and teach you through the experience? How did it make you a better leader?

5. What promise(s) from God do you need to declare over your life right now?

8

EMBRACE RECOVERY
AND RESTORATION

*There is something infinitely healing in the repeated
refrains of nature—the assurance that dawn comes
after night, and spring after the winter.*

RACHEL CARSON

I n leadership, it's important to seek an end to conflict. While much
of leadership is about dealing with conflict, we should not see conflict as the ideal or normal state. Yes. Leaders deal with conflict on
a regular basis. That's to be expected in a fallen world full of broken
and sinful people. If we lead with a mentality to obey God and pursue
his vision for us, we will come up against opposition. That being said,
God is gracious and brings many of our conflicts to a resolution. As
leaders, we seek for an end to the fighting and the chance to move
people forward.

God answered Jehoshaphat's prayer and gave Judah victory over her enemies without the Israelites having to raise a single sword. God had struck down Judah's enemies; not one of them had escaped. After the Israelites collected spoils from the enemy, the king assembled his people in the Valley of Beracah (lit. "blessing") to praise the Lord and rejoice in their victory. 2 Chronicles 20:27-30 shows us what the victorious return to Jerusalem looked like for Judah:

> Then they returned, every man of Judah and Jerusalem, and Jehoshaphat at their head, returning to Jerusalem with joy, for the LORD had made them rejoice over their enemies. They came to Jerusalem with harps and lyres and trumpets, to the house of the LORD. And the fear of God came on all the kingdoms of the countries when they heard that the LORD had fought against the enemies of Israel. So the realm of Jehoshaphat was quiet, for his God gave him rest all around.

After every great battle, there needs to be a time for recovery and restoration. Judah enjoyed the spoils of battle and praised God for delivering them. They entered a period of peace and rest from conflict.

To be sure, new conflicts will arise and the fighting will resume. But for a time, you can recuperate and prepare yourself (and those that follow you) to be ready and equipped for the next conflict. As a leader, this time is important, because it allows you to assess the conflict and make new plans and strategies moving forward. Failing to assess a conflict and plan for the future shows that you really didn't learn anything from the experience. It's one thing to fight valiantly on the battlefield. It's quite another to take steps to prevent a major conflict that puts you right back in the fight.

DEBRIEF THE CONFLICT

After you celebrate the end of a conflict, take the necessary measures to assess it from a personal and organizational perspective. A post-conflict assessment gives everyone the opportunity to reflect on what happened and how it was handled. If you hope to equip yourself (and those that follow you) for the next battle, this is essential. As a leader, you are responsible to initiate this and put it into action.

First, make a thorough assessment of your leadership throughout the conflict:

- What have you learned about yourself and leadership through the conflict?
- Where did your strengths come out in conflict? What about your weaknesses?
- If you had to experience the conflict over again, would you have done anything differently?
- How will those in your organization benefit from this conflict?
- What lessons does God want you to learn from the conflict? How will you implement them in your leadership?

This is a time for you to be honest with yourself. Ask God to reveal anything you might have missed in your personal assessment. Be transparent and allow him to expose anything you might be holding back. There are lessons to be learned in every conflict. Also, consider the work that God did in you through the conflict and how you're a stronger leader after the fight:

- What stories can you recall that confirmed God was leading you in the fight?
- How did he reveal himself and his purposes to you?
- How will this conflict's resolution advance God's kingdom?

Once you've made your assessment, share it with your team of confidants and those closest to you. They stood beside you in the conflict and can agree or even disagree with your assessments. Give them permission to be completely honest in their assessment, because they can offer fresh insights into your leadership that you wouldn't have otherwise. Poor leaders refuse this kind of assessment; they think they're above it because of their position. Great leaders welcome constructive criticism, because they know it makes them a better leader.

After assessing your leadership, assess the conflict from an organizational perspective. Invite others into the conversation and organize debrief sessions with your team of confidants and leaders in your organization. As thoroughly as possible, look at the conflict and its resolution from all angles:

- How did the leadership perform in the face of conflict? In what ways was the leadership united in working together to see the conflict come to an end? In what ways was it not?

- What team strengths were revealed through the conflict? What team weaknesses were revealed?
- How might the leadership improve and be better prepared for the next conflict? What plan does the leadership need to implement to ensure that these improvements are made? What are the possible consequences if the team fails to do this?

This organizational assessment is an open forum discussion that's moderated by you, the leader. Facilitate the discussion in such a way that encourages honesty and the free exchange of ideas. Revisiting the conflict may be uncomfortable at times, but it's a necessary step in recovery. Be prepared for heightened emotions and potential disagreement among leadership. When there is disagreement or contention, address it quickly, hear both sides and ask the group to give their opinion on the matter.

Ultimately, you want to move the discussion towards making a tangible plan with action steps and measurable goals. The plan should address ways to prevent major conflicts in the future and how to address any that do arise. As far as it depends on you, work to create a unified front and plan that equips the leadership for future battles. Think of the plan as the grease that gives your leadership movement going forward.

You have been given the task of leading your organization out of conflict and into a season of recovery and restoration. Just as you showed commitment to stay in the fight during conflict, commit to walking with those who follow you through this next season. As much as you were courageous in taking a stand to see God's vision fulfilled, show care, compassion and wisdom in leading those in your organization towards healing and restoration.

After the conflict ended at The Luke and we entered our own season of recovery, construction of our new facility began across town. The conflict had caused some to leave the church. Those that remained supported us, but it was clear that there was much pain and grief to address. After the leadership had assessed the damages, we knew the church needed two things to move forward: 1) unity in the congregation, and

2) time to heal and learn from the conflict. And we saw these two as connected—unity would cultivate healing and reflection and vice versa.

Amazingly, the church continued to grow at a rapid rate after the conflict. But our facility at the time simply couldn't accommodate the growth. We needed to come up with a plan to address the growth, because our new facility wouldn't be completed for another year. If we didn't address the issue, we were likely to lose a lot of people that didn't want to fight the crowds and congestion or be turned away because we maxed out our capacity.

The best option for us was to rent out a larger facility and meet there for weekly services. I gathered data on our attendance from three years back to demonstrate our growth pattern. I presented this option and data to the church's leaders and they voted. It was unanimous. They voted in favor of moving the weekly services to a much larger rented facility until the new church was completed.

Meeting at another facility required an enormous amount of volunteer help from The Luke's members. What started out as a small group of volunteers, swelled into an army of committed members who believed in God's vision for the church. Every Sunday they would arrive at 5:00 a.m. and set up for our services. The *espirit de corp* of those volunteers was infectious and exciting to watch. They worked together—as one—to make things happen in the church. Their hard work and dedication was a wonderful witness to me. We weren't just a community of believers, we were a *family of faith* that was willing to sacrifice for one another.

> GREAT LEADERS WELCOME CONSTRUCTIVE CRITICISM, BECAUSE THEY KNOW IT MAKES THEM A BETTER LEADER.

Our members sensed the importance of what was taking place at the church. This temporary move was only a stepping-stone. We were confident that greater things were to come. That confidence was uniting us in powerful ways to see the bigger picture. The storm of conflict had done its damage to the church, but our people were willing to help pick up the pieces and rebuild a safer, stronger house of worship. We lived out the story of Nehemiah in our conflict. Now, we were living out his story in our rebuilding.

This newfound energy in the church showed me that God was driving his vision home in our congregation. His vision wasn't just for a new building with more space and amenities. It was to call a people to do great things and think big about their God. It was to shake off small-minded faith and seek greater growth and fruit in the church for the sake of the kingdom of God.

FINDING FORGIVENESS

The ability to forgive others is the distinguishing and indispensable quality of Jesus' followers. In his Sermon on the Mount, Jesus makes it clear to us that forgiveness is a requirement, not a request: "If you forgive others their trespasses, your heavenly Father will also forgive you, but if you do not forgive others their trespasses, neither will your Father forgive your trespasses" (Matt. 6:14-15). There is freedom in forgiveness, because it releases you from bitterness and anger towards those that wronged you. Forgiveness strips the enemy from sowing seeds of contempt and hatred. That isn't to say that forgiveness is easy. On the contrary, forgiveness can be difficult. Its difficulty lies in the fact that it's counterintuitive to our nature. We don't want to forgive others or even ourselves for sins committed. That's why Jesus was so revolutionary when he called his followers to love their enemies and pray for them (Matt. 5:44). It's far more difficult to hate someone if you pray for them.

Refusing to forgive others will keep you from fulfilling God's vision for your life. I cannot overstate the importance of this truth. A lack of forgiveness keeps us locked in the past and unable to move forward, because we continue to dwell on past wrongs and wounds. It takes faith and maturity to release those that have wronged you to the Lord and forgive them. It's important to acknowledge the seriousness of an offense, but leave room for God to do his work and do your part to love those who've wronged you. Paul speaks to this radical approach in Romans 12:18-20 when he says:

126

Beloved, never avenge yourselves, but leave it to the wrath of God, for it is written, "Vengeance is mine, I will repay, says the Lord." To the contrary, "if your enemy is hungry, feed him; if he is thirsty, give him something to drink; for by so doing you will heap burning coals on his head." Do not be overcome by evil, but overcome evil with good.

The sting of an offense can last for a long time. I understand that all too well. After the conflict ended at The Luke, my thoughts lingered on those who had wronged me. As much as I wanted to move on, the pain was still there. I didn't want to let go of it, because, in a strange way, I thought that doing so would invalidate the pain and rejection I suffered. But how could I ask others to forgive if I wasn't willing to do it myself? Eventually, I came to see that forgiveness was necessary if I hoped to experience healing. Moreover, without forgiveness I couldn't be the leader I needed to be in the aftermath of our conflict.

Holding on to the pain and refusing to forgive others will cause us to sulk in self-pity. No one wants to follow a leader who's self-absorbed in his or her own world of pain. As leaders, we acknowledge the pain and ask God to give us direction and change our embittered hearts. The memories of past hurts may not disappear altogether, but you can choose to focus your mind on greater things and allow God to heal those wounds. Don't allow these painful memories to live in your head rent-free. Send them an eviction notice that reads:

I choose to dwell on whatever is true, honorable, just, pure, lovely, commendable and anything that is excellent and worthy of praise (Phil. 4:8-10). Jesus has forgiven me and asks me to forgive others. I choose to live in the light of his forgiveness and not stay in the darkness of bitterness and hate. I will rejoice in God's forgiveness and forgive others for wronging me. I choose to live in the freedom of God's wonderful grace!

TRUSTING OTHERS

Going through conflict can affect your trust of others. In my case, it was difficult to trust others because that trust had been betrayed severely in the conflict. Nevertheless, I could not compromise the relationships in my life over a lack of trust. I had to learn to trust again. You might have to do the same in the aftermath of a major conflict.

If you can't trust people in your organization, you're likely to resort to micromanagement. I've not met one person who enjoys someone looking over their shoulder all the time. Micromanaging is an ineffective form of leadership, because it stifles freedom and creativity in the workplace. Simply put, people can't perform at a high level if they sense that you don't trust them. As you look to bring restoration to your organization, you must communicate trust. This is a deal breaker. If trust isn't communicated, distrust will spread like a cancer throughout your organization. I've seen paranoid leaders that think everyone is out to get them. It's tragic, really, because their lack of trust not only affected them, but everyone they encountered. On the other hand, I've also seen leaders exhibit enormous trust in others. Their followers actually *wanted* to work hard for them, because of the trust endowed to them. I think it's truly remarkable what people are capable of if you give them responsibility and communicate that you trust them. Give others the benefit of the doubt until they prove you wrong. That's the best policy to prevent you from becoming a leader that lacks trust.

> WE MUST LEARN TO HAVE CONFIDENCE IN THOSE WE'VE PUT ON OUR TEAM AND THOSE WHO ARE IN LEADERSHIP WITH US.

Your trust is especially important for your team of confidants. Those closest to you need your confidence; they want assurance that you believe in them. A story where distrust had disastrous consequences is found in 1 Kings 12. The story takes place after King Solomon's death. Everyone gathered in Shechem to make Solomon's son, Rehoboam, Israel's next king. During Solomon's reign, he had placed a heavy tax burden on the Israelites to pay for his palaces and public projects. The people appointed a man by the name of Jeroboam to represent them before the new king in hopes of easing their burden. Jeroboam went before the king and said, "Your father made our yoke heavy. Now therefore lighten the hard service of your father and his heavy yoke on us, and we will serve you" (12:4). Rehoboam asked Jeroboam to return in three days for a response.

The king first went to the older men in his leadership for counsel. These elders advised Rehoboam to honor the people's request. However, the king didn't trust their advice and sought the counsel of his younger, less experienced friends instead. They advised Rehoboam to respond to the people by saying, "My little finger is thicker than my father's thighs. And now, whereas my father laid on you a heavy yoke, I will add to your yoke. My father disciplined you with whips, but I will discipline you with scorpions" (12:10-11).

On the third day, Rehoboam answered the people's request as his friends had advised him. The people were outraged and rebelled against the king. Ten of Israel's tribes seceded from the nation, splitting the kingdom in two. It was, in every sense of the word, a fiasco. Never again would Israel be united as it was under David and Solomon.

Rehoboam's distrust cost him dearly. His legacy is forever tainted by his foolishness to not put his confidence in the wisdom of Israel's elders. As a leader, he failed miserably. Not only did he pay the price for his error, but all Israel suffered as well. Rehoboam's story is a cautionary tale for leaders. We must learn to have confidence in those we've put on our team and those who are in leadership with us.

FIND NEW RHYTHMS AND ROUTINES

Coming down from a major conflict means that you must reestablish a sense of normalcy in your organization. When you're engaged in battle, your senses are heightened and you're on alert at all times. We're made to respond that way when we find ourselves in a dangerous situation. That's why God gave us adrenaline. However, that's a temporary response; it cannot be sustained. Sooner or later, you have to get back to daily life and responsibilities. Otherwise, you run the risk of causing yourself physical and mental fatigue (or worse) and wearing down those around you.

When a conflict ends, work to find new rhythms and routines for your organization. Make it clear that the fighting has ceased and that you've entered a new season of recovery and restoration. Communicate this with your words and actions. How you find new rhythms and routines will depend on your organization. Ask the question, "What one routine could we put in place this week/month that would most improve life in the organization?" Practice it and see what happens. When the next week/month rolls around, implement another routine. Examples of these might include having a regularly scheduled time for devotion and prayer in the morning before the workday starts or forming teams to tackle specific projects rather than assign them to individuals. Overall, your role as a leader is to reestablish stability and functionality in the organization, offer counsel to those who need healing, and guide your organization out of day-to-day combat and into the peace God has given you.

STAYING HEALTHY

Maintaining emotional, physical and spiritual vitality is essential for leadership. If you're going to lead your organization effectively in and out of conflict, you have to stay healthy. To do this, you need to exercise self-care, seek necessary counseling and establish healthy boundaries.

Self-care includes the deliberate steps you take to maintain overall health. Exercising self-care glorifies God, because it reflects our belief that the body is "a temple of the Holy Spirit" (1 Cor. 6:19). If you believe your body is the Spirit's dwelling place, you will do everything you can to keep it honorable and clean for him. If not, you may fall prey to addictions, poor eating habits, laziness and self-destructive behaviors. As a leader, it's important to model a healthy lifestyle. Self-care will make you a better leader who's more mentally alert and physically fit. It will also enrich your relationships and maximize your productivity in life and work.

We are holistic people, which means there is a connection between what our mind thinks and how our bodies function. As an example, look at the possible physical effects of depression on a person. They range from fatigue to insomnia to cancer. The mind has an enormous effect on the body. That's why it's important for us to heed Paul's admonition to "take every thought captive to obey Christ" (2 Cor. 10:5).

Maintaining overall health must address our physical, emotional and spiritual needs. There are a number of important areas to address in exercising self-care. First, get the proper amount of sleep. God gave you sleep so you can recharge your mind and body daily. Don't take this for granted. In our industrious and ambitious culture, it's tempting to sacrifice sleep to meet the demands of our busy schedules. But sacrificing sleep comes with consequences, which range from irritability to more serious health problems. Neuroscientist and sleep expert Russell Foster says that:

> Sleep is the golden chain that ties health and our bodies together [...] If you have good sleep, it increases your concentration, attention, decision-making, creativity, social skills, health. If you get sleep, it reduces your mood changes, your stress, your levels of anger, your impulsivity, and your tendency to drink and take drugs.[1]

Along with getting enough sleep, it's essential to have a balanced, nutritional diet. As the old saying goes, "You are what you eat." So, instead of consuming fatty and processed foods, introduce more lean proteins, fruits, vegetables and complex carbohydrates into your diet. Avoid foods high in salt and sugar. You don't have to go overboard here. It's okay to enjoy fried foods once in a while. Have that slice of cake. The key here is self-discipline and moderation in choosing to regularly eat foods that are good for you and making things like fast food the exception, not the norm. It's remarkable how having self-discipline in your diet affects your self-discipline in other areas.

Physical exercise is another component of self-care. I suggest carving out time in your schedule two to three times a week to go to the gym or get outside and sweat. You don't have to become a gym rat, but you need to burn off some energy (and calories). This is especially true for those with more sedentary jobs who sit at a desk for eight hours a day or more. Physical exercise boosts your energy, fights disease and improves your overall mental health and mood. It keeps you sharp as a leader. Along with enough sleep and a good diet, it can also reduce stress and anxiety.

Exercise your mind and stay mentally active. A stimulated mind will go a long way in maintaining good health. Research has shown that, "more frequent cognitive activity across the life span has an association with slower late-life cognitive decline [e.g., Alzheimer's disease]."[2] Whether young or old, be a life-long learner. There's no shortage of fascinating things in this world to occupy your mind. Read, write, pick up a new hobby, go back to school, play challenging games. Do what you need to do to stay curious and engaged mentally.

Learn the value of play. As a leader, you're committed to your people and your responsibilities. You're highly ambitious and you want to achieve great things. That's wonderful and God honoring. But don't go through life huffing and puffing to get things done, only to realize that you never took time to enjoy life's pleasures. Having visited many people on their deathbed, none of them ever told me they wished they had worked more. There's more to life than work. Enjoy life and learn to take a break and play.

> LAUGH TOGETHER AND CELEBRATE LIFE. DON'T LET IMPORTANT MOMENTS PASS YOU BY.

I've had to learn to take a break and get away in order to make sure I stayed healthy as a pastor. When my wife and I go on vacation, I leave work behind and unplug completely. I need to step outside of the concerns and distractions of work and enjoy life more simply. My church won't fall apart if I need to get away, rest and recharge; I've entrusted my congregation to leaders who can shoulder the load until I return. If you exercise self-care, you'll know when it's time to work and when it's time to play.

As a leader, you need to spend time with your friends and family. Laugh together and celebrate life. Don't let important moments pass you by. No amount of money, prestige or accolades will buy back lost opportunities to enjoy the precious moments and important relationships in your life.

An often-overlooked aspect of self-care for leaders is having healthy boundaries. As a leader, you have a lot of responsibilities and you're asked to care for the needs of those in your organization. But those in your in organization also have responsibilities. When there's confusion between what's my responsibility and what's your responsibility, you have a lack of boundaries. In his book *Boundaries: How to Say Yes, How to Say No to Take Control of Your Life* (Thomas Nelson Publishing: 1992), Henry Cloud speaks to the importance and function of boundaries:

> Boundaries define us. They define what is me and what is not me. A boundary shows me where I end and someone else begins, leading me to a sense of ownership. Knowing what I am to own and take responsibility for gives me freedom. Taking responsibility for my life opens up many different options. Boundaries help us keep the good in and the bad out. Setting boundaries inevitably involves taking responsibility for your choices. You are the one who makes them. You are the one who must live with their consequences. And you are the one who may be keeping yourself from making the choices you could be happy with. We must own our own thoughts and clarify distorted thinking.[3]

Leaders (especially those in the pastorate) that lack boundaries get caught in the cycle of always needing to address the next issue. Their motivation may be to care for others, but they end up taking on the responsibilities and concerns others are responsible for.

Some leaders suffer from a kind of 'messiah complex' where they think the organization's success depends solely on them. That's why they have their hand in the cookie jar of every department in their organization in an attempt to control every decision. Besides needing to eat a big slice of humble pie, those leaders also need to learn how to delegate responsibilities and trust others to perform their duties.

Establish definite boundaries in your organization. Communicate roles and responsibilities clearly for everyone. When those boundaries are violated, address the issue lovingly and encourage those who follow you to own up to what they are responsible for. Every healthy and successful organization has set boundaries for their people to understand their role to play and how it works to achieve the organization's purpose and goals.

SEEKING PROFESSIONAL CARE

If you're experiencing prolonged issues related to anxiety, depression or unresolved emotional wounds, I recommend seeking professional care.

Unfortunately, many in Christian circles have stigmatized counseling and therapy. They tend to offer a number of advisable solutions, such as "Just read your Bible and pray more." "Volunteer more." "Pick up another small group." The answer is not to do more but to seek help in the right places.

Along with his Word and prayer, I believe God has also given us professionals who are experienced and trained at diagnosing and treating particular mental and emotional issues. We go to the doctor if we sense something is wrong with us physically and doesn't go away. The doctor diagnoses the problem and gives us a prescription to address it. So what's wrong with going to a counselor if your depression doesn't pass?

TO BE AN EFFECTIVE LEADER, YOU HAVE TO BE EMOTIONALLY, PHYSICALLY AND SPIRITUALLY HEALTHY.

Ignoring the fact that you have unresolved emotional wounds will not make them go away. Stuffing those emotions will only lead to more problems down the road. To avoid further injury, share your struggle with those closest to you and seek the right kind of professional care. You may need to see a counselor once a week. That's okay. You're brave for admitting you have a problem and addressing it. You may need to change your routine to include better self-care. Again, you're brave for taking the steps necessary to protect yourself, your family and those in your organization.

After the conflict at The Luke ended, I was riding high for a time. God had given us victory and his vision was approaching fulfillment. But something wasn't right with me. Something just didn't sit well.

As a pastor, I was spending much of my life caring for and listening to others by making myself available to them. Unfortunately, I wasn't doing the same for myself. I would come home weighed down by a heavy heart and unresolved pain and think, "I don't want to burden my wife with these problems." So I kept them locked inside.

Change came when my wife and other people close to me started to see my issues manifest themselves. They encouraged me to talk to a counselor. In truth, I was doing my family and congregation a disservice by not seeking professional care. So I began seeing a counselor once a week. During our sessions I was able to unlock those feelings and give voice to past hurts and fears. I discovered that the real problem wasn't what they had done to me, but what I was doing to myself by holding on to so much pain and bitterness. Not only did seeing a counselor benefit me emotionally with healing and restoration, it reinvigorated my leadership strength and purpose.

To be an effective leader, you have to be emotionally, physically and spiritually healthy. Therefore, evaluate your self-care strategies and whether you're doing what's necessary to be a healthy leader. Make sure you have boundaries set up in your personal and professional life. And don't let pride get in the way if you (or others) see that you need to seek professional care.

EMBRACING REST

Jesus had one of the most demanding schedules as a leader. As an itinerant preacher, he traveled from town to town teaching, healing and caring for others. Can you imagine the massive crowds that followed him and how many of them demanded his attention? Not only that, he was also discipling twelve men and preparing them to carry on his ministry after he left earth. Jesus kept himself busy during his ministry.

Here's the interesting thing. Despite the constant demands of his ministry, Jesus found time to rest. Like us, he knew what it was like to grow weary, and he needed to get away, recover and recharge regularly.

Scripture records multiple instances where Jesus rested. Mark 6:30-31 tells us that, "The apostles returned to Jesus and told him all that they had done and taught. And he said to them, 'Come away by yourselves to a desolate place and rest a while.'" In John 4:6, we find Jesus resting at a well before his conversation with the Samaritan woman, because he was weary from his journey. Jesus even fell asleep in the stern of a ship in the middle of a raging storm at sea (Mark 4:35-41).

Not only do we see Jesus taking time to rest in Scripture, he also offers rest to the weary and burdened. Jesus invites his followers to enjoy true rest in him: "Come to me, all who labor and are heavy laden, and

I will give you rest. Take my yoke upon you, and learn from me, for I am gentle and lowly in heart, and you will find rest for your souls. For my yoke is easy, and my burden is light" (Matt. 11:28-30).

Are you weighed down by the demands of leadership? Does life seem to have you by the tail, tossing you from one place to the next? Take heart and find true rest in Jesus. Jesus needed rest and he knows that you need it too. That's why he offers you the best rest possible—his own. What does it mean to find rest in Jesus? It means taking your cares and concerns to him rather than holding on to them. It means taking the pains, burdens and disappointments of life (past and present) and giving them to him. It means bringing the responsibilities and demands of leadership to him and saying, "I need help, Lord. I trust that you're in control and will give me what I need to be a good and effective leader for you."

THE ENEMIES OF REST

There are no greater enemies to rest than stress, worry and anxiety. If we're being honest, we put too much faith in our worries. Why do I say that? Consider how much time we spend worrying about something. Many of us operate under this strange delusion that worrying actually helps us. Otherwise, we wouldn't devote so much time to it.

Worry and anxiety cause us to lose perspective on what's important and what truly matters in life. We spend our time and mental energy thinking about things—big and small—that may or may not happen. How many of the things that you worry about actually happen? My guess would be very few.

No leader can lead effectively operating under the influences of worry and anxiety. Anxiety causes us to freeze up in the face of our worries and can be paralyzing and extremely detrimental to your leadership.

One of the consequences of confronting conflict was extreme stress. As a result, I developed high blood pressure that threatened my health. When my doctor told me I had high blood pressure, I saw it as a red flag in my leadership. The fight was putting me under unnecessary stress and causing me to worry and be anxious about the present and the future of our church. I needed to make changes to address the things that were holding me back from being an effective leader at The Luke.

Another way we deceive ourselves when it comes to worry is to think there are things in life worth worrying over—as if we have a worry allowance that we can use on certain things like our health, finances, family, etc. Should we be concerned about our health, finances and family? Absolutely. Does that concern give us permission to worry needlessly over them? No.

Jesus doesn't leave any room for stress, worry and anxiety in the life of his followers. In Matthew 6:27-33, Jesus tells us exactly how he feels about worry and anxiety and how we are to respond to them:

> [W]hich of you by being anxious can add a single hour to his span of life? And why are you anxious about clothing? Consider the lilies of the field, how they grow: they neither toil nor spin, yet I tell you, even Solomon in all his glory was not arrayed like one of these. But if God so clothes the grass of the field, which today is alive and tomorrow is thrown into the oven, will he not much more clothe you, O you of little faith? Therefore do not be anxious, saying, "What shall we eat?" or "What shall we drink?" or "What shall we wear?" For the Gentiles seek after all these things, and your heavenly Father knows that you need them all. But seek first the kingdom of God and his righteousness, and all these things will be added to you.

God knows you and he knows what you need in the face of an uncertain situation or difficulty. If you have time to worry, you have time to pray. Spend your time wisely—go before the Lord to "cast all your anxieties on him because he cares for you" (1 Pet. 5:7). Don't fall into the trap and think you have any reason to worry or be anxious in life.

Worrying doesn't change your situation. God does. He's a good God who doesn't want you to doubt his goodness towards you. Worry says, "God can't." God says, "I can. Don't worry. Trust me, because I'm a good Father." Embrace the promise of Jesus that your heavenly Father loves you and cares for your needs when you bring them to him (Luke 11:9-13).

NOW IS THE TIME

Coming out of conflict and into a time of recovery and restoration takes time. It doesn't happen overnight. Thankfully, God has given you a number of resources to help you transition your organization into a time of peace. Assess the conflict from a personal and organizational perspective. Make a plan to prepare for the next conflict. Begin the process of healing and restoration. Recover by making self-care and rest a priority in your life and leadership. Don't give the enemies of stress, worry and anxiety an advantage. Fight them by seeking true rest in Jesus and seeking his kingdom above all. Now is the time for you to rest and recover. Take care of yourself and those in your organization.

The path you take towards fulfilling his vision isn't always pleasant and God will ask you to sacrifice much in the process. You will suffer loss in your journey. Of that much I am sure. You may lose relationships or financial stability or even your job. Your enemies might drag your name through the mud. But the difficulty and the sacrifice are for your good, and they serve God's ultimate purpose. That is a rock solid promise from Scripture: "And we know that for those who love God all things work together for good, for those who are called according to his purpose" (Rom. 8:28). Let the sweetness of that promise wash over you. Let it give you hope that God never wastes an experience; that he uses *all* of your story to bring about good and wonderful results.

DISCUSSION QUESTIONS

1. Think about a major conflict you've encountered in the past and assess it from a personal and organizational perspective. Consider the evaluation questions mentioned in the 'Debrief the Conflict' section of this chapter.

2. What new rhythms and routines could you introduce in your organization to improve your organization's health?

3. On a scale of 1-10, how would you rate your self-care? What changes do you need to make to have better self-care?

4. What's your personal view on seeking professional care from a counselor? Do you think it's necessary? Why or why not?

5. What in your life causes you the most stress, worry or anxiety? How does it affect your leadership? What about your relationships? How could you address this worry a different way?

9

PORTRAIT OF A GREAT LEADER

If your actions inspire others to dream more, learn more,
do more and become more, you are a leader.

JOHN QUINCY ADAMS

Here we are at the end of our journey together. I trust that you've picked up some valuable lessons in reading this book, and I trust God will use those lessons to improve and enhance your leadership in powerful ways! Looking back, I see how God was using the pain, difficulty and hardship of our conflict at The Luke to tell a greater story about himself. If you get anything from this book, I hope it's this: God's vision comes with God's provision.

As a leader, my journey was hard, and there were times when I wondered why God put me (and our church) through it. What I came to see is that the path I took in leading others through conflict was well worn. Many leaders have walked it before me, and many leaders will walk it after I'm long gone. Great leaders will come and go in the passage of time and circumstance. What remains constant as leadership passes from one leader to the next is the God who calls and equips.

Moses is remembered as one of the greatest leaders in Scripture. God called him to lead the Israelites out of slavery in Egypt, through the wilderness and into the Promised Land. However, in a fit of anger at Meribah, Moses disobeyed God and was disqualified from entering the Promised Land with the rest of the Israelites (Num. 20:2-13). Because of this, leadership would pass from the elder Moses to the younger Joshua.

Before the Israelites entered the Promised Land, the covenant between God and his people was renewed at Moab. Moses took this occasion to address the people and remind them where they had come from and where they were going. He reminded them of their identity as God's chosen people and implored them to choose life and live for God and not themselves. If they chose God, they would be blessed. If they chose their own path, they would be cursed. In Deuteronomy 30:15-18, Moses tells the people:

> See, I have set before you today life and good, death and evil. If you obey the commandments of the LORD your God that I command you today, by loving the LORD your God, by walking in his ways, and by keeping his commandments and his statutes and his rules, then you shall live and multiply, and the LORD your God will bless you in the land that you are entering to take possession of it. But if your heart turns away, and you will not hear, but are drawn away to worship other gods and serve them, I declare to you today, that you shall surely perish. You shall not live long in the land that you are going over the Jordan to enter and possess.

Moses' words are both encouraging and sobering. He understood the life and death matter at hand for the Israelites. Israel had a defining choice before them, and Moses wanted them to choose God. Moses' farewell address was his way of calling the Israelites to stand, because they were about to embark on a dangerous and conflict-filled journey. He would not go with them, but he knew their success would depend on their faith in God, not themselves.

There wasn't anything in the Israelites that deserved God's love and affection. As a nation, they were small and insignificant. But God remembered his covenant with their fathers and his promise to bless the offspring of Abraham (Gen. 15). He made a promise and swore by his own name to make Israel a great nation. And he promised to give them victory in their conquest of the Promised Land. All that was required of Israel was to obey and trust their God.

You also have a choice in your leadership. If God has given you a vision, he expects you to obey and trust him in pursuing it. He's given you precepts for godly leadership in his Word and from others who have taught you. He's also given you experience as a teacher to help you distinguish between good and poor leadership. Again, God's vision comes with his provision. So, choose to honor God in your leadership and you can't lose. Things won't always work out the way you expect them to, but they will always work out for your good and serve as a witness to the God you serve.

> WHAT REMAINS CONSTANT AS LEADERSHIP PASSES FROM ONE LEADER TO THE NEXT IS THE GOD WHO CALLS AND EQUIPS.

As we near the end of our time together, I wanted to give you some final thoughts and reflections on leadership. My goal in this chapter is to show you what it looks like to live *for* God's glory as a leader, how to live *in* that glory and what it looks like to teach others to do the same.

Think of this chapter as God's portrait of a great leader. Let this portrait be something you display prominently and look at often. Admire the craftsmanship of God's handiwork. See the knowledge and skill behind every brushstroke. Notice the attention to detail and the painstaking care it took to create a work that inspires others and fills them with a sense of awe. Great leaders of vision do that for God; they reflect to the world who God is and what he's like.

Like Moses, I want you to choose God in your leadership and pursuits. If you want to be successful in leadership, you must not overlook what is addressed in the pages of this book. Through this book I'm passing on my story and leadership principles to you. There's truth in these words and I hope you will act on it. The truth lies not in me, but in the Source of all truth. So, be a doer—not just a hearer—of God's Word! (James 1:22-25).

GIVE GOD GLORY IN YOUR SUCCESS

God deserves all the glory in your story and in your success. So, be intentional about putting him out front when you celebrate your victories. He gave you (and those in your organization) the strength and perseverance to accomplish his vision. Many, both within and outside, will look at you as a leader and attribute your success to your own abilities. They will laud you with compliments and praise for a job well done. When that happens, take the opportunity to shift the focus off you and on to God. Don't be disingenuous; be emphatic and remind others that the only reason for your success is that God called you and equipped you to achieve his vision.

One of the problems we have today in our culture is hero worship. We love stories where a hero comes to save the day. I think that's something God has ingrained in us. Just about every good book or film speaks to the desire for a hero's rescue. And we look for heroes in all kinds of places. Unfortunately, we often look for our heroes in the wrong places. The next time you go to the grocery store, take a look at the magazine isle. What you'll find on the covers of those magazines is an exhibition in hero worship. Celebrities. Athletes. Musicians. Politicians. Our longing for heroes is everywhere, even in the church. That's why I could not be more serious about giving God the spotlight when he gives you success in leadership.

Sooner or later, our "heroes" will let us down. Martin Luther once said, "Men at their best are at their best men." Nearly every leader in the Bible had at least one major flaw that revealed his brokenness. Abraham's fear caused him to lie to Abimelech and say Sarah was his sister, not his wife (Gen. 20). Jacob deceived his father into giving him his blessing instead of Isaac's eldest son, Esau (Gen. 27). Moses' anger led him to murder one of Pharaoh's servants (Ex. 2:11-12). David abused his power to commit adultery with Bathsheba and tried to cover it up, which led to the murder of Uriah, Bathsheba's husband

(2 Sam. 11). Peter's cowardice caused him to deny the Lord three times (Matt. 26:33-35).

Scripture shows us that there's only one Hero, and that's God. In Jesus, God is the ultimate Hero of our story. He is the same yesterday, today and forever (Heb. 13:8). He is the valiant Hero that never fails us. He was never overcome by temptation and completed God's mission in perfect obedience to the Father at his First Coming. Revelation 19:11-16 gives us a picture of Jesus' heroic return to finally defeat his enemies and establish God's kingdom as the King of kings and Lord of lords.

God is the Hero of the story and we are to bring him glory with our leadership. Don't just pay lip service to this truth. Back up your words with your actions. Don't say, "To God be the glory" and spend the rest of your time talking about all your accolades and accomplishments. Our goal as leaders is not to make our name great and have it on the side of the building one day, but to make God's name great and point others to him and his salvation.

Remember: the world is watching you as a leader. To whom will they attribute your success, to you or to God? Don't let hubris be your downfall as a leader. Help others see the truth of where your success lies. Take a stand and give God the glory!

SEEING GREATER PURPOSE

Understanding the purpose behind a conflict is important to us as leaders. If you've endured great hardship and difficulty in a conflict, chances are you've asked God, "Why?" at some point during or after the fight. We want answers to confirm that our cause is worthy and merits a fight. If we feel confirmed in the fight, we will be emboldened to press on. If we don't feel confirmation, we might think we'd be better off blowing the whistle, calling the game and hitting the showers.

The truth is you may not understand the purpose behind a conflict for some time. After the battle has ended, it may take weeks, months or even years to see the greater purpose behind it. While wanting to know the purpose behind a conflict is understandable, it's not as important as seeing the conflict as an opportunity for a deeper knowledge and experience of God.

To illustrate this point, let's look at the story of Job. God tested Job's faithfulness by allowing Satan to attack him. Job lost everything and experienced an incredible amount of suffering because of his enemy's attacks. His suffering was so great that even Job's wife tells him to curse God and die so the torment would stop. But Job remained strong and faithful and did not curse God (1:22).

Job's three friends tried to give him a reason for his suffering; they thought God was punishing Job for something he did. Job rebuked his friends and demanded to speak to God directly and get an answer for his suffering. God does respond to Job's request, but in a different way. Instead of answering him, God delivers two speeches that contain a series of questions that relate to God's unmatched power and sovereignty (38-41). Job is silenced before the Lord. When he finally speaks, he confesses that the Lord's purposes will not fail and that he presumed to think beyond his own knowledge: "I know that you can do all things, and that no purpose of yours can be thwarted. 'Who is this that hides counsel without knowledge?' Therefore I have uttered what I did not understand, things too wonderful for me, which I did not know" (42:2-3). In the end, God restored Job and gave him back twice what he had before.

> GOD IS THE HERO OF THE STORY AND WE ARE TO BRING HIM GLORY WITH OUR LEADERSHIP.

What is the point of Job's story and why does it matter to your leadership? The point is this: God wants you to trust his character in the midst of conflict. When you don't have all the answers, it's easy to doubt your leadership. "Have I done something wrong?" "Why is this happening to me?" People in your organization may ask you these same questions. You need good theology to respond to these questions when they come. Let God's Word remind you who God is. The Bible tells you God is good, which means he never acts out of cruelty or malice. The Bible tells you that God is trustworthy and able to keep his promises. The Bible tells you that God is all-knowing, which means he understands your suffering and the reasons behind your conflict.

The Bible tells you that God is all-powerful, which means nothing can keep him from fulfilling his purposes. The Bible tells you that God has the same control over your situation as he does over the motion of the sea and the rising of the sun. Honestly, we have no reason to doubt his character, even in the midst of great conflict and suffering.

God gives you guidelines to live by in pursuit of his vision for you. He doesn't give you the entire script of the story. In Scripture, God never gave any of his leaders a play-by-play of everything that was going to happen in their journey. Instead, he gave them a vision. Sometimes God's vision is made clear to you from the beginning. Other times it becomes clearer as events in your life transpire. What's important for you, as a leader, to remember is that obedience and trust are necessary when answers don't seem to come in an intense conflict.

DETERMINE WHAT'S NEXT

So you've fulfilled the vision God has given you. You've poured your heart into his vision and the long hours, hard work and sacrifice have finally paid off. You've celebrated your victory and given God praise for it. You've assessed the conflict and allowed time for healing and recovery. Now what?

First, don't get too comfortable. While God gives you time to rest from the conflict, it may not be long before he calls you into something new. God works in his own timing, so we don't know when a new call will come. We can't set a timeline for a new vision, but we can prepare ourselves to receive it.

How do you prepare to receive a new vision? By staying in communion with the Lord. Put yourself in the right posture to receive. Spend time with him and with God's people. Listen for his voice. Jesus said, "My sheep hear my voice, and I know them, and they follow me" (John 10:27).

One afternoon, I was at a local park near my house. The sun was out, which meant there were a lot of kids out there running around and doing what kids do best—playing. I watched them as they laughed and got lost in their little imaginations. From behind me I heard a mother yell, "Sweetie! Come on. It's time to go." As soon as she said that, a small child (he couldn't have been older than four or five) perked his head up out of the crowd. He turned around, saw his mother and ran to her. He knew his mother's voice and was able to pick it out from all the others.

That's the kind of familiarity you need with your heavenly Father. Do you know his voice? Do you spend time to become familiar with it? Are you regularly in his Word, reading and meditating on it? Are you going to him with your daily concerns and requests? Do you spend time worshiping and fellowshipping with God's people? If so, his voice is becoming more familiar to you.

Second, be prepared to chart a new course in life and leadership. A new vision will bring new adventures and changes. Anticipate challenges and conflict to come with them. Because you've gone through conflict, you've gained more experience, wisdom and know-how as a leader, and God used the conflict to shape you into a stronger, more equipped leader.

You can't predict what the next vision will look like. God may call you to change careers. He may call you to leave and move to another city or country. Or he might call you to stay where you are and serve faithfully in your organization for the next twenty years. No two stories are alike, and God wants us to embrace the uniqueness of our story and how he is working through it. Avoid comparing your story to others'. That only leads to envy and discontentment. Take ownership of your story as one only God could tell through you!

Know your strengths and weaknesses as a leader. If you've done your homework to assess your leadership in conflict, you know where you need work. New visions come with new changes and challenges. New conflicts won't look like the old ones. Therefore, it's important to be adaptable as a leader. Lead from your strengths but be open to stretching yourself and making adjustments to your leadership. A new conflict may require you to strengthen your public speaking skills. Or it might mean that you have to take on more administrative responsibilities. There's no shortage of examples here. What's key to understand is that great leaders learn how to best adapt to new dynamics and circumstances. They still lead from the core strengths God has given them, but they also know how to bend and move as new conflicts arise.

Keep your eyes fixed on the ultimate goal in your leadership. Regardless of what God calls you to do next, he has set this goal before you—to do God's work and bring light into a dark world. It doesn't matter what kind of leadership position you have, you're called to focus on this goal above all others, whether you're a pastor, a mechanic, a housewife, a doctor, a garbage collector or a schoolteacher. This goal is achievable in every kind of leadership. Let Paul's testimony encourage you to seek the ultimate prize in Christ Jesus:

> Not that I have already obtained this or am already perfect, but I press on to make it my own, because Christ Jesus has made me his own. Brothers, I do not consider that I have made it my own. But one thing I do: forgetting what lies behind and straining forward to what lies ahead, I press on toward the goal for the prize of the upward call of God in Christ Jesus. (Phil. 3:12-14)

LEADERSHIP TRAITS

There are a number of characteristics that distinguish great leaders from poor leaders. Many of those characteristics have been discussed in this book, but I would like to highlight a few more that I think are essential. When we fill a new position on our leadership team at The Luke, I'm looking for these essential traits. I ask myself whether I see these traits in this leader or whether this person is putting up a front. Whether face-to-face in an interview or based on their track record in leadership, I want to see these characteristics lived out in a leader.

FIRST, DO THEY HAVE CONVICTION?

I want to see passion in their eyes when they talk about their life, hopes and dreams. I want to see that they've acted on their convictions in leadership; that they've not just held on to dreams, but have actually put things into motion to achieve them.

SECOND, DOES THIS LEADER SEE HIS OR HER FLAWS?

A leader may understand his or her strengths, but do they also see where they're weak? Knowing your weakness is actually a strength in leadership. That's because leadership is something you're always improving upon, and it requires constant assessment and adjustment to your character. You might be redeemed, but you're still prone to pride, pettiness and selfishness.

God doesn't call the equipped. He equips the called. We may look at God's leaders in Scripture as spiritual giants, but the truth is they needed as much work as we do. Consider the apostles; they were a ragtag group of mostly uneducated, unskilled and ordinary men. They didn't necessarily have the pedigree of great leaders as we define it today. They were also given to poor judgment, bad attitudes and completely misunderstanding Jesus. And, yet, Jesus called them, trained them, equipped them and sent them out into the world to change it. John MacArthur once remarked that, "Our Lord uses ordinary, weak, failing, ignorant saints. Guess why. [Because those are] the only kind there are. Welcome to the group."[1] God uses flawed and broken people to reach a flawed and broken world. A leader who refuses to see this fact is least likely to be honest and work to address any character flaws.

> GOD USES FLAWED AND BROKEN PEOPLE TO REACH A FLAWED AND BROKEN WORLD.

THIRD, IS THIS LEADER A RISK TAKER?

Put another way, does the leader have what it takes to put it all on the line in pursuit of God's vision? Rarely—if ever—do people achieve great things by playing it safe. Great leadership demands some element of risk taking. I'm looking for leaders who aren't afraid to try something new or challenge the status quo. I'm also looking for someone who isn't afraid to fail. Failure happens in leadership. What you do with failure and how you bounce back from it is the difference maker. That doesn't give a leader license to be foolish and careless in their position. But, by wisdom and experience, a leader should be able to know when risk is necessary and called for.

That being said, you can't really risk with God. Take a moment to consider the source of your calling in leadership. It's God, right? Does he have all power and authority to see his vision become reality? Yes. Can anyone or anything keep him from accomplishing his purposes? No. Will you learn more about God and grow as a leader whether an outcome is successful or not? Yes. Is your measure of success and failure the same as the world's? No. So, if God gives you a vision and equips you to fulfill it, how in the world can you lose? You can't, which means that your risks aren't really risks after all.

FOURTH, IS THIS LEADER A GRACE GIVER AND RECEIVER?

When this person fails, do they see that there's grace and forgiveness? Does this leader understand that, "The steadfast love of the LORD never ceases; his mercies never come to an end; they are new every morning" (Lam. 3:22-23)? Great leaders see their constant need for grace, know how to receive it and move on. In the same way, great leaders know how to give grace. In leadership, those who follow you will fail in one way or another. Do you have the compassion to address that failure and be grace-filled in your approach? Great leaders know when a rebuke is necessary—but they also know how to extend grace and to leave someone feeling encouraged, rather than shamed. Someone's failure might even result in their termination, but that doesn't mean the conversation can't still be filled with grace.

FIFTH, DO I SEE THIS PERSON'S LIFE BEARING FRUIT?

A person can impress you with their words, but those words need to be verified by actions. I'm looking for someone whose life is a testimony (not a denial) of their calling as a leader. Jesus said, "By this my Father is glorified, that you bear much fruit and so prove to be my disciples" (John 15:8). Leadership is more than a title. It's a lifestyle. Great leaders live out their leadership to make those around them better. Not just better in a productive, utilitarian way, but in an all-around way that seeks for real change and growth.

If you want a cheat sheet for seeing whether you're a fruit bearing leader, look no further than Galatians 5:22-23 and Paul's description of the Fruit of the Spirit: "But the fruit of the Spirit is love, joy, peace, patience, kindness, goodness, faithfulness, gentleness, self-control;

against such things there is no law." Do you see these characteristics in your leadership? Do others see them in the way you treat others and how you conduct yourself as a leader? When faced with a major conflict, use the Fruit of the Spirit as a gut check for your leadership. If you don't see evidence of these, it's time to reevaluate your leadership and make some changes.

DISCIPLESHIP: TEACHING THE NEXT GENERATION TO STAND

Having considered these five leadership traits, I want to address one more. When I'm recruiting a new leader to join our team, I want to see teaching and mentoring ability in that leader. *Does this leader have enough foresight to understand the need to equip the next generation to lead?* Are they prepared to invest the time and energy to disciple others as Jesus did?

Discipleship is an intentional relationship you enter into that is characterized by calling, teaching, equipping and sending. That's the model Jesus used with his disciples, and no one's come up with a better model since. Discipleship was Jesus' way of passing on leadership to his followers. We are called to do the same in our leadership.

As a leader, consider how you might be a disciple-maker in the lives of those around you. Discipleship happens in everyday life and relationship. Therefore, you need to know who you're discipling. Get to know their background, their family, their personality, their strengths and their weaknesses. Discipleship doesn't happen from the stage or the pulpit. It doesn't happen in seminars. That's preaching and teaching. They may have discipleship aspects, but it's not the kind of discipleship we see in Jesus. Jesus lived among his disciples and engaged with them in a personal way.

For three years, Jesus taught his disciples daily, listened to their stories and showed patience in their ignorance and lack of maturity. All the while, he was training and equipping them to take the reigns of his church after he was gone. Jesus' method of teaching and equipping involved some on the job training too. We see this in Luke 10:1-20 when Jesus sends out seventy-two of disciples ahead of him with specific instructions. Before he sent them, he said to them, "The harvest is plentiful, but the laborers are few. Therefore, pray earnestly to the Lord of the harvest to send out laborers into his harvest" (10:2). Great leaders know how to pass on their leadership to a new generation.

If you hope to have a healthy organization, you need to be actively engaged in raising up new leaders to share the load of responsibility. Leaders who fail to do this tend be insular in their leadership; they prefer to lead from a distance and isolate themselves. They may have an inner circle assisting them, but their motivation is not to relinquish control and entrust others who are quite capable of leading. Organizations with that kind of leadership fail when their leader leaves or is dismissed.

This should give leaders pause to ask a few questions. First, "Am I taking the right steps to ensure that my organization will carry on without me?" Second, "Am I actively engaged in training up new leaders through personal discipleship?" Third, "In that discipleship, am I giving them responsibility and am I giving them room to grow as leaders who aren't dependent on me?"

As mentioned earlier, discipleship is something that happens in everyday life. It's not a class; it's a lifestyle. As a leader, you're intentional about picking leaders to disciple. But these disciples must be teachable and willing to learn, work hard and stay with you throughout the entire process.

An important part of discipleship is casting vision for your disciple. Help them develop a picture of the kind of leader they want to become. At the beginning of the process, ask your disciple:

- What do you want to learn from all this?
- How do you want to grow as a leader? What skills do you want to develop? What character traits do you want to work on?
- What do you want to be different about your character and leadership in a year's time?

Listen intently to them and take notes. Understand their motivations and desires in leadership. If you understand them, it will greatly enhance your ability to teach and equip them.

We don't learn to become a great leader in a vacuum. We need hands-on experience. Therefore, give your disciples opportunities to develop their leadership with real responsibilities and consequences. We treat practice differently than the way we treat the actual game when the score counts.

Will there be failure and misunderstanding alone the way? Yes. But take those failures and misunderstandings and use them as teachable moments. They are wonderful opportunities for growth. Give them the chance to have another crack at it and learn from their mistakes. Sometimes we have to learn the hard way by failing and trying again. This is where your patience and commitment as a leader are essential.

DISCIPLESHIP WAS JESUS' WAY OF PASSING ON LEADERSHIP TO HIS FOLLOWERS.

As you disciple, keep in mind those who taught you and helped you to be the leader you are today. They had to be patient with you and give you second, third and fourth chances to get it right. Do the same for those you disciple and make them leaders who will make leaders. By doing this, you're making a leadership chain that will be strong for future generations.

There's a Greek proverb that says, "A society grows great when old men plant trees whose shade they know they shall never sit in." There's a lot of truth to that statement, especially in discipleship. It's not all about us. As leaders, we need to have a present and future mindset. We need to be the best leader possible for our organization in the present. We also need to have vision and look into the future to tomorrow's leaders. Are you making leaders that make other leaders? Are you preparing the next generation for the conflict and challenges ahead?

As you disciple, you need to have a kingdom mindset. With a vision of God's kingdom, Jesus provided a new way of living for his disciples. In discipleship, we show this new way to our disciples as well. In Matthew 5-7, Jesus gives his followers a portrait of kingdom life, which is life as God intended. His Sermon on the Mount included teachings on: blessing (5:1-12), reconciliation (5:21-26), faithfulness (5:27-37), love and service (5:38-6:4), prayer and fasting (6:5-18), investing in eternal treasure (6:19-21), trusting God (6:25-34), judging others (7:1-5), approaching God (7:7-11) and the Golden Rule (7:12). Teach and live out this mindset in your leadership. I'm confident your disciples will thank you for it. You will also have made them better leaders in the process.

A FINAL EXHORTATION

Martin Luther King Jr. once said, "The ultimate measure of a man is not where he stands in moments of comfort and convenience, but where he stands at times of challenge and controversy." Dr. King faced conflict in his pursuit of God's vision. He took a stand before the giants of ignorance, injustice and racism. Although he died in pursuit of his vision, his legacy lives on. The same can be said for countless other leaders that refused to back down in the heat of conflict.

In a chapter that's come to be known as the 'Hall of Faith,' the author of Hebrews illustrates faith in action by chronicling the lives of past saints. Hebrews 11 gives us testimony after testimony of men and women who took a stand. Not only did God give them the strength to stand, he gave them a vision of greater things. Of Abraham it is said: "By faith he went to live in the land of promise, as in a foreign land, living in tents with Isaac and Jacob, heirs with him of the same promise. *For he was looking forward to the city that has foundations, whose designer and builder is God*" (11:9-10 [italics added]).

In light of this wonderful witness to true faith, the author draws our attention to the One that gives us hope that we can stand in great conflict:

> Therefore, since we are surrounded by so great a cloud of witnesses, let us also lay aside every weight, and sin which clings so closely, and let us run with endurance the race that is set before us, looking to Jesus, the founder and perfecter of our faith, who for the joy that was set before him endured the cross, despising the shame, and is seated at the right hand of the throne of God. (Hebrews 12:1-2)

As a leader, you will face conflict. When it comes, there will be no confusion as to what you are to do. I pray that you will apply the precepts and principles of this book into your leadership. I pray bless-ings on your efforts. May God be with you in the storms of conflict and may he assure you with his promise and power. May his vision come to pass in your life and leadership. May God allow you to stand!

I close with one of my favorite songs by Donnie McClurkin, entitled 'Stand.' May his words be an encouragement to you in the darkness of night when the conflict rages on and you wonder whether you have the strength to carry on. Remember: the night is always darkest before sunrise.

Stand and be sure
Be not entangled in that bondage again
You just stand and endure
God has a purpose,
Yes, God has a plan
Tell me what do you do when you've done all you can
And it seems like you can't make it through?
Child, you just stand, you just stand, stand
Don't you dare give up through the storm,
Stand through the rain
Through the hurt,
Yeah, through the pain
Don't you bow, and don't you bend
Don't give up, no, don't give in
Hold on,
Just be strong,
God will step in
And it won't be long

Keep standing my friend!

DISCUSSION QUESTIONS

1. Having read this book, what kind of changes do you need to make to your leadership? What kind of leader do you want to become?

2. What's the biggest challenge or conflict you're currently facing in leadership? How might the biblical principles and truths of this book help you to stand?

3. Consider the seven leadership traits mentioned in this chapter and evaluate your leadership by them. Which of the seven is your strongest trait? Which of the seven is your weakest? Why?

4. Are you presently discipling other leaders? If not, what is holding you back? If so, what benefits do you see in discipling leaders?

ENDNOTES

INTRODUCTION

1. Robert E. Quinn describes trial-by-fire crises of leadership that purify our character and leadership ability. These situations bring out our 'Fundamental State of Leadership,' which reveals certain aspects of our leadership that don't come out unless there is intense conflict. "[M]y colleagues and I have found that when leaders do their best work, they don't copy anyone. Instead, they draw on their own fundamental values and capabilities—operating in a frame of mind that is true to them yet, paradoxically, not their normal state of being. I call it the fundamental state of leadership. It's the way we lead when we encounter a crisis and finally choose to move forward." Robert E. Quinn, "Moments of Greatness: Entering the Fundamental State of Leadership," *Harvard Business Review* (July-August 2005): 3-4.

CHAPTER ONE

1. Daniel Goleman highlights the importance of a leader using multiple styles of leadership: "[N]ew research by the consulting firm Hay/McBer, which draws on a random sample of 3,871 executives selected from a database of more than 20,000 executives worldwide, takes much of the mystery out of effective leadership. The research found six distinct leadership styles, each springing from different components of emotional intelligence. The styles, taken individually, appear to have a direct and unique impact on the working atmosphere of a company, division, or team, and in turn, on its financial performance. And perhaps most important, *the research indicates that leaders with the best results do not rely on only one leadership style; they use most of them in a given week—seamlessly and in different measure—depending on*

the business situation [italics mine]." Daniel Goleman, "Leadership that Gets Results" *Harvard Business Review* (March-April 2000): 3.

CHAPTER TWO

1. Chris Lowney has found the Jesuit model for leadership refreshing for today's leadership culture: "Founded in 1540 by ten men with no capital and no business plan, the Jesuits built, within little more than a generation, the world's most influential company of its kind. [...] Some elements of the Jesuit approach are increasingly finding validation in recent research—for example, the link between self- awareness and leadership. [...] What has been most revolutionary and most refreshing for me personally is that these principles address one's whole life and not merely one's work life. The Jesuits' principles made the company better because they made individual Jesuits better. Their principles are rooted in the notions that we're *all* leaders and that our whole lives are filled with leadership opportunities. [...] Jesuits eschewed a flashy leadership style to focus instead on engendering four unique values that created leadership substance: self-awareness, ingenuity, love and heroism. In other words, Jesuits equipped their recruits to succeed by molding them into leaders who: understood their strengths, weaknesses, values and worldview; confidently innovated and adapted to embrace a changing world; engaged others with a positive, loving attitude; and energized themselves and others through heroic ambitions." Chris Lowney," *Heroic Leadership: Best Practices from a 450-year-old Company That Changed the World*, Reprint ed. (Chicago: Loyola Press, 2005), 5-9.

2. Daniel Goleman, "Leadership that Gets Results" *Harvard Business Review* (March-April 2000): 8.

3. Ibid., 9.

CHAPTER THREE

1. Craig E. Runde and Tim A. Flanagan define this type of conflict as *task or cognitive conflict*, which "focuses on issues and can result in open and rigorous debate of problems." Craig E. Runde and Tim A. Flanagan, "Conflict Competent Leadership," *Leader to Leader*, Winter 2008, 47.

2. According to Runde and Flanagan, another type of conflict is *relational or affective conflict*, which "focuses on finding out who's to blame for a problem

more than (or instead of) how to solve it. [...] Relationship conflict has been shown to lead to poorer team results and morale." Ibid., 47.

3. Kenneth W. Thomas encourages leaders to take a proactive approach to address conflict directly and quickly in order to produce greater productivity in the workplace: "Managers reported spending 18% to 26% of their time dealing with conflicts, depending on their organizational level. That is a huge investment of time—the equivalent of many millions of dollars of payroll in moderate-sized to large organizations. Any significant improvement in the efficiency of conflict management—by surfacing conflicts quickly and directly and settling them cleanly—will produce productivity gains that far outweigh the cost of most conflict management programs." Kenneth W. Thomas, "Making Conflict Management a Strategic Advantage," *CPP, Inc. (Consulting Psychologists Press)*, 1.

4. With the Walt Disney company as her example, Suzy Wetlaufer encourages leaders to leverage conflict in constructive ways: "Disney comes out with at least two products a week, from new rides at the theme parks, to TV shows and movies, to CD-ROMs, to Little Mermaid makeup kits. How does all that innovation happen? This whole business starts with ideas, and we're convinced that ideas come out of an environment of supportive conflict, which is synonymous with appropriate friction. We create a very loose environment where people are not afraid to speak their minds or be irreverent. They say what they think, and they are urged to advocate strongly for ideas. That can be very noisy. It can be hard, too, because when you're loose, you say a lot of things, you challenge, you cajole, you provoke. Uninhibited discussion gets ideas out there so that we can look at them and make them better or just get rid of them if they don't work." Suzy Wetlaufer, "Common Sense and Conflict," *Harvard Business Review*, January-February 2000, 11.

5. Craig E. Runde and Tim A. Flanagan highlight three key qualities needed for a team to handle conflict. The first is *fostering trust and safety*. "Each person needs to feel that the other team members have his or her best interests in mind, or at least that they won't take advantage of him or her. Team leaders can foster trust in teams by serving as a model and making themselves vulnerable." The second is *developing strong collaboration*. "When team members work together closely, share information openly, and make decisions collaboratively, their sense of togetherness grows and they are better able to address the differences that arise." The third is *enhancing emotional intelligence within the team*. "Team leaders who want to create the right climate for addressing conflict need to stay aware of the emotional temperature in their teams. If they sense that team members are upset about an issue, it is important for them to address the matter and not let it fester."

Craig E. Runde and Tim A. Flanagan, "Hidden Potential Embracing Conflict Can Pay Off for Teams," *LIA* 28, no. 2 (May/June 2008): 10.

CHAPTER FIVE

1. Napoleon Hill, *Think and Grow Rich*, revised ed. (Chichester: Capstone, 2011), 213.

2. Paul Tripp, "You Talk to Yourself," *Paul Tripp Ministries, Inc.* (Wednesday's Word), February 26, 2014.

CHAPTER SIX

1. Richard Warren, *The Purpose-Driven Life: What On Earth Am I Here For?* (Grand Rapids, MI: Zondervan, 2002), 29-34.

2. T. D. Jakes, *Instinct: the Power to Unleash Your Inborn Drive* (Nashville, TN: FaithWords, 2014), 155.

3. George J. Kienzle and Edward H. Dare, *Climbing the Executive Ladder: A Self-Training Course for People Who Want to Succeed,* (New York: McGraw-Hill, 1950), 100.

4. Beth Laurie Jones, *Jesus, Entrepreneur: Using Ancient Wisdom to Launch and Live Your Dreams,* (Crown Business, reprint, 2002), 67.

5. Linda Hill and Kent Lineback view trust as the foundation of great leadership and influence. "Management begins with you, because who you are as a person, what you think and feel, the beliefs and values that drive your actions, and especially how you connect with others all matter to the people you must influence. Every day those people examine every interaction with you, your every word and deed, to uncover your intentions. They ask themselves, "Can I trust this person?" How hard they work, their level of personal commitment, their willingness to accept your influence, will depend in large part on the qualities they see in you. Trust is the foundation of all forms of influence other than coercion. You need to foster it." Linda Hill and Kent Lineback, "Are You a Good Boss – Or a Great One?," *Harvard Business Review* (January-February 2011): 7.

CHAPTER SEVEN

1. Stan Guthrie, *All That Jesus Asks: How His Questions Can Teach and Transform Us* (Grand Rapids, Mich.: Baker Books, 2010), 177.

2. "There has to be a certain letdown of pretense before the creativity flows. And you get that when you've been in the same clothes, in the same room, with the same turkey sandwiches getting dry in the same corner for a long time. I'm told even the Beatles had to play and play and play before they found their real creativity, their own style. Back in the early 1960s, even before they had Ringo Starr, when Pete Best was on drums, they would go to Hamburg, Germany, to make a living at little waterfront bars, and they would play every day, 18 hours straight to exhaustion. They were the C act at a lot of little places. They started out imitating Elvis; then they'd imitate someone else and someone else. Eventually, they were so exhausted, they couldn't copy anyone else, and they became themselves. They became the Beatles." Suzy Wetlaufer, "Common Sense and Conflict," *Harvard Business Review* (January-February 2000): 10.

3. Richard J. Foster, *Celebration of Discipline: the Path to Spiritual Growth*, 20th ed. (San Francisco: Harper San Francisco, 1998), 103.

CHAPTER EIGHT

1. Russell Foster, "Why Do We Need Sleep?" (lecture, TEDGlobal 2013, Edinburgh, Scotland, June 2013).

2. Robert S. Wilson, Patricia A. Boyle, et al., "Life Span Cognitive Activity, Neuropathologic Burden, and Cognitive Aging," *Neurology* 81, no. 4 (July 23, 2013): 314-21.

3. Henry Cloud and John Townsend, *Boundaries: When to Say Yes, How to Say No to Take Control of Your Life*, Revised ed. (New York: Thomas Nelson Publishing, 1992), 35.

CHAPTER NINE

1. John MacArthur, "Twelve Ordinary Men" (sermon, Grace Community Church, Sun Valley, California, July 19, 2015).